BLOOMSBURY CURRICULUM BASICS

Teaching Primary RE

BLOOMSBURY CURRICULUM BASICS

Teaching Primary RE

**By
Naila Missous**

BLOOMSBURY EDUCATION
LONDON OXFORD NEW YORK NEW DELHI SYDNEY

BLOOMSBURY EDUCATION
Bloomsbury Publishing Plc
50 Bedford Square, London, WC1B 3DP, UK
Bloomsbury Publishing Ireland Limited
29 Earlsfort Terrace, Dublin 2, D02 AY28, Ireland

BLOOMSBURY, BLOOMSBURY EDUCATION and the Diana logo are trademarks of Bloomsbury Publishing Plc

First published in Great Britain, 2025 by Bloomsbury

This edition published in Great Britain, 2025 by Bloomsbury

Text copyright © Naila Missous, 2025

Illustrations copyright © Dave Smith, 2025

Naila Missous and Dave Smith have asserted their rights under the Copyright, Designs and Patents Act, 1988, to be identified as Author and Illustrator of this work

Bloomsbury Publishing Plc does not have any control over, or responsibility for, any third-party websites referred to or in this book. All internet addresses given in this book were correct at the time of going to press. The author and publisher regret any inconvenience caused if addresses have changed or sites have ceased to exist, but can accept no responsibility for any such changes.

Every reasonable effort has been made to trace copyright holders of material produced in this book, but if any have been inadvertently overlooked the publishers would be glad to hear from them.

All rights reserved. No part of this publication may be: i) reproduced or transmitted in any form, electronic or mechanical, including photocopying, recording or by means of any information storage or retrieval system without prior permission in writing from the publishers; or ii) used or reproduced in any way for the training, development or operation of artificial intelligence (AI) technologies, including generative AI technologies. The rights holders expressly reserve this publication from the text and data mining exception as per Article 4(3) of the Digital Single Market Directive (EU) 2019/790.

A catalogue record for this book is available from the British Library

ISBN: PB: 978-1-8019-9581-8; ePDF: 978-1-8019-9582-5; ePub: 978-1-8019-9584-9

2 4 6 8 10 9 7 5 3 1 (paperback)

Text design by Marcus Duck

Typeset by Newgen KnowledgeWorks Pvt. Ltd., Chennai, India
Printed and bound in the UK by CPI Group Ltd, CR0 4YY

To find out more about our authors and books visit www.bloomsbury.com
and sign up for our newsletters.

For product safety related questions contact productsafety@bloomsbury.com

Online resources accompany this book at: www.bloomsbury.com/BCB-Teaching-RE

Please type the URL into your web browser and follow the instructions to access the resources.
If you experience any problems, please contact Bloomsbury at: companionwebsite@bloomsbury.com

Contents

Introduction ix
RE in your classroom xiv

Part 1: Key Stage 1 1
1   The disciplinary skills 2
2   Substantive knowledge: The Abrahamic faiths 5
3   Judaism 7
4   Christianity 18
5   Islam 28

Part 2: Key Stage 2 37
6   The disciplinary skills 38
7   Judaism 42
8   Christianity 50
9   Islam 56

Part 3: The Dharmic religions 69
10   Introducing the Dharmic faiths 70
11   Hinduism – Sanatana Dharma 73
12   Sikhi – Sikh Dharma 81
13   Buddhism and Jainism 89
14   Creating links between faiths 92

Part 4: Other approaches 97
15   Introducing Humanism 98
16   A worldviews approach 104

Glossary 111
Bibliography 117

Introduction

Religious education (RE) in primary schools can vary in presentation and display; however, the foundations have similar links across all schools. Religious education is referred to in a variety of ways, such as RE, RS (religious studies) or simply religion. At times, it is even blended with other subjects to fit a school's timetable. What is essential to remember is that, for maximum impact, RE should be a standalone subject – that is to say it has benefit on its own and value in its own right, and is a key component of a school's curriculum and development.

Despite the importance of religious education, as a subject it is not part of the National Curriculum. It is, however, compulsory for all state-funded schools in England to teach RE, although parents do have a legal right to withdraw their children from RE lessons.

The decision on how RE must be mapped out as part of a school's curriculum depends on whether a school is an academy, faith or local authority school and so forth, along with the local SACRE (Standing Advisory Council for Religious Education), which will be discussed later in the book.

What is substantive knowledge in religious education?

In the context of RE in primary school education, substantive knowledge refers to the essential content and information that teachers are expected to teach and that pupils learn about with regard to different religions and worldviews. Worldview here relates to the idea that religions and philosophies start and exist with people: how they think, interact and adapt in life with a faith – or none.

Substantive knowledge goes beyond simply knowing facts and involves a deeper understanding of the beliefs, practices, rituals and key concepts associated with various religions, giving all pupils, from Key Stage 1 through to Key Stage 2, the credit that they deserve when it comes to understanding and applying new knowledge.

The Department for Education provides a framework for RE in primary schools, and it outlines the substantive knowledge that pupils should acquire during their education (DCSF, 2010). The essential substantive knowledge that matches up with the content of the subject typically includes the study of major world religions such as Christianity, Islam, Hinduism, Sikhism, Judaism and Buddhism, as well as exploring secular worldviews and ethical issues. This is usually in conjunction with the work of local SACRE boards, whose work also influences the outcomes of curriculum design in many schools.

A SACRE is an independent statutory body made up of people from a wide range of faith groups who volunteer to be members. Every local authority is required by law to have a SACRE.

The key functions of a SACRE include: supporting schools by providing advice on teaching and the choice of teaching materials; monitoring standards; and supporting the effective provision of collective worship and teaching through the agreed syllabus (a syllabus that sets out what all schools in a local authority – with the exception of voluntary aided schools – should include in their RE programme of study). A SACRE will review the agreed syllabus every five years, to allow for consideration of new research, demographic changes in the local area and any new educational thinking that will aid teaching. There can be variations and influence from the SACRE syllabus if a school is an academy.

RE in a school with a religious character must be provided in accordance with the beliefs of the religion or denomination to which the school ascribes. The school may also offer RE aligned with a local agreed syllabus and include teachings about other faiths if it chooses.

Substantive knowledge in RE often covers topics such as:

1. **Beliefs and teachings**: Understanding the core beliefs and teachings of different religions, including the concepts of God, creation, the afterlife and moral guidelines.
2. **Practices and rituals:** Learning about the religious practices, rituals and ceremonies associated with various faiths, such as prayer, worship, festivals and rites of passage.
3. **Sacred texts:** Exploring the sacred texts of different religions, such as the Bible in Christianity, the Quran in Islam, the Vedas in Hinduism and the Torah in Judaism.
4. **Places of worship:** Studying the architecture and significance of places of worship in different religions, such as churches, mosques, temples and synagogues.
5. **Key figures:** Understanding the lives and teachings of key figures within each religion, such as Jesus Christ in Christianity, Prophet Muhammad (PBUH) in Islam and Buddha in Buddhism.
6. **Ethical and moral issues:** Examining ethical and moral principles within different religions and considering how these principles guide individuals in making ethical decisions (particularly in Key Stage 2).

Substantive knowledge in RE aims to foster respect, tolerance and understanding of diverse religious and non-religious perspectives. It provides pupils with a foundation for engaging with and critically reflecting on the beliefs and practices of others, contributing to their overall cultural and religious literacy, while also working in cross-curricular harmony across other humanities subjects.

Primary schools provide excellent cultures and environments for this to have an impact, particularly with the advantage of (predominantly) one teacher delivering the majority of the subjects to the same class, repeatedly. This means that teachers are able to make purposeful links, so that children can also make links across their learning. An example of this would be a map in the classroom that is used in geography lessons. The use of the map not only offers a visual representation of human geography, but also provides the opportunity to locate where religions or philosophies began and to see the journey links between religions – for example, how the Abrahamic religions all fall within the same region of the world – as well as allowing for the exploration of ancient religions, thus making links to history.

What is disciplinary knowledge in Religious Education?

Disciplinary knowledge in RE in English primary school education refers to the skills, methods and approaches that teachers use as the underlying threads when teaching, which then aid pupils to develop, understand, analyse and engage with religious and non-religious ideas (substantive knowledge).

Disciplinary knowledge involves the application of critical thinking, research skills and the ability to evaluate information in the context of the study of religion. The aim is to go beyond rote memorisation of facts and to encourage pupils to think analytically and critically about religious beliefs, practices and issues. This is where the marriage between the substantive and disciplinary knowledge comes into play.

Key elements of disciplinary knowledge in RE are personal to a school's general curriculum outline, but may include the following.

1. **Critical thinking:** Encouraging pupils to think critically about religious and ethical questions, enabling them to evaluate different perspectives and develop their own reasoned opinions. This can sometimes come under the SACRE-suggested threads of 'Exploring' and 'Connecting'. A 'thread' refers to a recurring theme or concept that connects different lessons, topics or subjects over time. Think of it like a consistent idea woven through various learning experiences, helping pupils to build deeper understanding. For example, a thread in history might be civil rights, explored in different historical contexts across different year groups. It is like following a storyline that grows and connects ideas as pupils learn more. In RE, the threads will do the same.

2. **Analytical skills:** Helping pupils to analyse religious texts, rituals and practices, considering their historical, cultural and social contexts. Making connections between different religions and worldviews, while also understanding their own rituals.

3. **Reflection and Expression:** Encouraging pupils to reflect on their own beliefs and values, as well as providing opportunities for them to express their thoughts and opinions on religious and ethical matters.

4. **Respectful dialogue:** Promoting respectful and open dialogue about religious and non-religious perspectives, fostering an understanding of diverse viewpoints and expressing this in a respectful manner.

By incorporating disciplinary knowledge in our RE teaching, we can aim to equip pupils with the tools to navigate and understand the diversity of beliefs and values in the contemporary world.

Foundation Stage	Discover	Which stories are special to some people? Why?
Key Stage 1	Explore	What is Christianity? What do Christians believe? What is Judaism? What do Jews believe? What is Islam? What do Muslims believe?
Lower Key Stage 2	Connect	What are different beliefs about God?
Upper Key Stage 2	Connect	Why do some people believe in God and some people do not?
Key Stage 3	Question	Is it necessary to prove that God exists?

The relationship between disciplinary knowledge and substantive knowledge in RE in English primary schools is cooperative. Both are essential components of a well-rounded RE education and curriculum, ensuring that pupils not only gain knowledge about differing religious traditions but also develop the skills needed to engage thoughtfully and critically with this knowledge, to take them beyond the primary school environment.

About this book

The suggestions and ideas presented in this book are grounded in my extensive experiences of working with an agreed syllabus, teaching RE in various educational settings and collaborating with colleagues across different key stages and secondary schools. These experiences have provided me with valuable insights into the diverse landscapes of RE education and have shaped the practical strategies and approaches shared in this resource.

Firstly, my involvement with agreed syllabi has afforded me a deep understanding of the curriculum frameworks and learning objectives that underpin RE education. By engaging with these documents, I have gained clarity on the essential concepts, themes and skills that should be addressed in RE lessons. This knowledge forms the foundation upon which the suggested activities and lesson plans in this book are built, ensuring alignment with curriculum requirements and educational standards. This means that teachers will be able to match up lesson ideas and strategies with the expectations of RE in their school context, area and agreed syllabus.

Furthermore, my experience of teaching RE in various contexts has equipped me with a nuanced understanding of the diverse needs, backgrounds and abilities of pupils. Whether teaching in urban, rural or multicultural settings, I have encountered a wide range of learners with unique perspectives and experiences. This first-hand experience has informed the development of differentiated teaching strategies and inclusive approaches to RE instruction, catering to the diverse needs of all pupils.

Introduction

Additionally, collaborating with colleagues across different key stages and secondary schools has provided me with a broader perspective on the continuum of RE education. By engaging in professional dialogue and sharing best practices with fellow educators, I have gained insights into effective pedagogical approaches, assessment strategies and curriculum innovations in RE. This collaborative ethos underscores the philosophy of this book, which seeks to draw upon collective expertise and foster a community of practice among RE educators.

RE in your classroom

What do I need to know?

What you need to know with respect to your disciplinary knowledge can be found in this book for your own learning and reference. The substantive knowledge will develop with time, as you map out your curriculum from key stage to key stage, making sure that links to skills such as questioning, making connections and experiences are found throughout all of your children's learning.

Teachers aiming for impactful RE will have several things to prioritise and consider, such as:

- What will my classroom look like?
- How will the work be presented?
- Is this communicated effectively to all of those teaching the subject in school?

Firstly, understanding the diverse backgrounds and beliefs of pupils is crucial. This necessitates creating a safe and inclusive environment where all perspectives are respected and valued. Secondly, teachers should strive for authenticity in their teaching, using accurate and unbiased information about various religions and belief systems. Thirdly, there should be room for different lenses and worldviews to be explored and for teachers, as well as children, to admit to their own personal biases and worldviews. Those are what make us all unique, after all!

All of this includes incorporating primary sources, guest speakers and field trips, where possible, to provide first-hand experiences. Additionally, teachers should foster critical thinking skills, encouraging pupils to analyse and question religious concepts, practices and their societal implications. Furthermore, promoting empathy and understanding among pupils is essential, in order to emphasise the common values and shared humanity across different religions and cultures. Lastly, teachers should recognise the transformative potential of RE, not only in imparting knowledge, but also in nurturing pupils' personal growth, moral development and ability to engage constructively with the world around them. By embracing these principles, teachers can cultivate an RE curriculum that is not only educational but also impactful in fostering tolerance, respect and appreciation for religious diversity.

This chapter will provide templates, example lesson resources and suggestions that can be incorporated in the lesson ideas that follow, and which will enable you to provide the best RE possible for your children and school.

How can it be presented?

Religious education in primary school can be presented through a variety of engaging and age-appropriate activities. As shown in some of the lesson examples in this book, one possible activity could be storytelling, which is a powerful method with which to introduce pupils to key religious narratives. The stories suggested in the lesson plan ideas, as well as the stories that you may source yourself, will be multi-use across key stages and lessons.

Hands-on activities like crafts, role-playing and cooking (even in the Early Years, for a sensory approach) can help children to explore religious rituals and traditions in a tangible way. They bring real life into the classroom.

Using multimedia resources such as videos, songs and interactive websites, especially in the digital age in which we're living, can enhance learning and cater to different learning styles. A virtual trip to a mosque or a Buddhist centre is one way of bringing this straight into your classroom!

Classroom discussions provide opportunities for pupils to express their thoughts, ask questions and learn from each other's perspectives. Trips to local places of worship or visits from guest speakers can offer first-hand experiences and promote community engagement.

Resource ideas

The following resource suggestions are referenced in the lesson plan ideas that feature in this book. They are designed to complement the lesson plans but can easily be integrated with your own lesson ideas. They are versatile, allowing for use across different year groups, and can be tailored to suit the unique needs and abilities of your pupils. Use these resources to enhance your lessons, provide additional context or support differentiated learning activities that engage all pupils effectively.

Question generator

A multi-use resource, this question generator can be adapted for each key stage, according to children's abilities. It is also an effective tool for challenging pupils. It could be used before receiving visitors, watching a film or reading a story, or it could even be used as a pre-assessment of learning, with the questions revisited at the end of the unit to analyse whether any of the pupils' questions have been answered. The range of question words prompts a mix of questions requiring substantive or disciplinary knowledge, and invites children to explore different aspects of religion. Using the words as a basis can help you come up with different questions which require children to look at their knowledge in varied ways.

The following grids have been populated with some example questions, but you should feel free to generate as many of your own questions as you see appropriate.

Key Stage 1 Question Generator

	is/was	does	should
What	What is the name of the cross in Christianity?	What did Moses do to help the Jewish people?	What should Jewish people make sure their food is?
When	When is a special holiday celebrated in your religion?	When does someone pray?	When should we help others?
Who	Who was Jesus?	Who did Moses spoke to when he was in Egypt?	Who should we help when people are in need?
Where	Where is the Kaaba located?	Where did God tell Moses to go to?	Where should a Christian pray?
Why	Why is fasting important to Muslims?	Why does prayer help some people to feel better?	Why should we be kind to each other like the Prophet Muhammad (PBUH)?

Key Stage 2 Question Generator

	is/was	does/did/do	should	would	could	if
What	What is the significance of the Quran in Islam?	What does Shabbat mean in Judaism?	What should we learn from the teachings of Jesus in Christianity?	What would a peaceful world look like according to Humanist values?	What could be learned from the teachings of Sikhism about equality?	What would you give zakat for if you were a Muslim?
When	When is the most important holiday celebrated in Islam and what does it commemorate?	When does a person who follows Judaism light the menorah and what does it symbolise?	When should Christians go to church and what do they do there?	When would a Humanist celebrate a significant life event, like a wedding or a naming ceremony?	When could a Hindu participate in a puja (worship ceremony) and what is the purpose of it?	When do Buddhists meditate and how does it help them in their daily lives if they practise it regularly?
Who	Who is Guru Nanak and why is he important to Sikhs?	Who does the Vedas say we should respect and honour in our lives?	Who should we help, according to the teachings of Christianity?	Who would Muslims look to for guidance in their faith and daily life?	Who could you talk to about your beliefs in Humanism?	Who would you seek wisdom from if you wanted to learn about Buddhism?
Where	Where is the Guru Granth Sahib kept by Sikhs?	Where does the concept of karma come from and how does it influence behaviour in Hinduism?	Where should Muslims visit on pilgrimage?	Where would you look for guidance on being a good khalifah (steward) in Islam?	Where could people practise the idea of ahimsa in daily life?	Where would someone pray if they were a Jain?

	is/was	does/did/do	should	would	could	if
Why	Why is the concept of Dharma important in Hinduism?	Why do Muslims pray in congregation?	Why should Christians practise forgiveness?	Why would a Muslim fast during Ramadan?	Why could going to a special place (like a church, temple or mosque) matter to people?	Why should we be respectful of each other's religions if we want to live in a peaceful community?
How	How is karma understood in Hinduism and how does it influence a person's actions?	How does the practice of prayer differ among Sikhs, Muslims and Christians?	How should a Muslim help others in the community?	How would a Humanist celebrate the birth of a child?	How could understanding Islamic teachings promote peace and tolerance in a diverse society?	How would your life change if you practised the teachings of Hinduism, such as ahimsa (non-violence)?

Scenario and knowledge cards

Scenario cards are versatile teaching tools used in RE lessons to present pupils with real-life situations that require them to apply their understanding of various beliefs and practices. By working through these scenarios, learners can engage in critical thinking and discussion, exploring how different religions would approach specific ethical dilemmas or life events.

Additionally, knowledge cards can be integrated into lessons to prompt learners to revisit key facts and concepts that they've previously studied. These cards can feature important terms, definitions and summaries, reinforcing pupils' understanding and aiding retention. Once again, some examples have been provided, but you can create your own, tailored to the learning on which you are focusing. It is even possible for your pupils to create their own cards and quiz one another.

The following example is suggested in Chapter 11 on Hinduism, although it is multifaceted and can be used across religions and key stages.

Helping a friend with homework	Sharing your lunch with a classmate	Lying to avoid getting in trouble	Cleaning up litter in the park
Bullying someone on the playground	Stealing a toy from a sibling	Being kind to a new pupil	Ignoring someone who needs help

Below are example cards for use when teaching Islam in Key Stage 1, followed by an adapted version for Key Stage 2. The former could be used as revision prior to your Key Stage 2 lesson.

Teaching Primary RE

Name the five pillars of Islam	The Arabic name for God	The holy book in Islam	The tower structures that form part of a mosque
The respected leader who leads prayer	The final messenger and prophet	The place of pilgrimage in modern-day Saudi Arabia	The month of fasting
Faith is integral to many Muslims. What's this called?	PBUH stands for...	SAW stands for...	Salah is Arabic for prayer. How many times a day is salah mandated?
How might Muslims show zakat?	The ummah can be described as...	The place of pilgrimage in modern-day Saudi Arabia is...	Ramadan is permitted for whom?

Maps

Geography and maps are invaluable in RE lessons as they provide a visual context for understanding the origins and spread of religions. Maps can show the geographical locations of sacred sites, pilgrimage routes and the distribution of religious communities worldwide. This helps pupils to grasp the global diversity and cultural significance of various faiths.

RE in your classroom

Using maps, pupils can explore how geography influences religious practices and traditions, such as how terrain and climate affect architecture and festivals. Additionally, studying the migration of religious groups enhances pupils' understanding of historical and contemporary issues related to religion, culture and society. Creating these cross-curricular links will lead to a tighter and more honed journey of learning for your pupils.

The use of maps can be as simple as using a map (digital or paper) on the classroom wall, so that every time a new religion or thought is introduced, it is located and pinned on the map.

Key Stage 1 and maps
Using maps in RE for Key Stage 1 pupils can be both educational and fun. Examples include:

- Use a simple, age-appropriate world map, highlighting countries in which major religions originated.
- Use colourful stickers or icons to mark significant religious sites, like temples, churches, mosques and gurdwaras.
- Incorporate storytelling by linking each location to a story from that religion, helping young children to make connections.
- Incorporate interactive activities, such as drawing lines on a map to connect religious symbols to their geographic origins.

This visual and hands-on approach helps young learners of all abilities to grasp the concept of global religious diversity and the importance of various places in different faiths.

Key Stage 2 and maps
During Key Stage 2, using maps in RE can involve more detailed and interactive activities, as well as incorporating the activities described above for Key Stage 1.

Examples include:

- Use world maps to trace the spread of religions over time, marking key historical events and routes, such as the spread of Buddhism along the Silk Roads. This also provides opportunities for cross-curricular links with history.
- Research and present on different religious sites around the world, using maps to pinpoint their locations and significance.
- Use interactive digital maps and online tools to explore religious demographics and cultural landmarks. This approach not only enhances geographical skills but also deepens understanding of the global impact and diversity of religious practices. There are many resources that allow visits to religious sites virtually!

Useful links:

https://retodaymagazine.online/article/unveiling-connections

Statistics

Using statistics in RE, particularly in Key Stage 2, can make learning more engaging, insightful and also real. Giving pupils tangible examples of minorities and majorities and percentages of communities in the UK and globally allows them to understand religions and worldviews on a real-life scale. It also adds a level of reality for them, as well providing opportunities for cross-curricular links with maths. Examples include:

- Use simple, relatable data, such as the number of adherents of major religions worldwide or within pupils' own area. This can then be expanded to compare this data with that of the country as a whole.
- Create colourful charts and graphs to visualise information, helping pupils to see the global diversity of faiths.
- Compare the religious composition of different countries or explore how religious demographics have changed over time.
- Integrate statistics into projects, like creating a classroom census of religious beliefs and traditions, if you feel that pupils are comfortable sharing these.

These activities not only enhance numeracy and data interpretation skills, but also encourage an appreciation of religious diversity and trends.

Prediction and analysis table

This table uses imagery or a quote as the central focus for the lesson, which is then mapped out against some questions and prediction space for pupils.

How might some followers of Sikhi use the gurdwara?	What inside a gurdwara signifies that it is a place of worship?

How can we link ideas of seva in the gurdwara to everyday life?	Does the gurdwara reflect all aspects of Sikh worship?

RE in your classroom

Here, children have focus questions to help them tailor their answers. It acts as a visual aid to which they can continually refer and also gives them space to make their own notes.

The following is an example I have used in the classroom:

How can we link these ideas of community to other religions?	How might these ideas influence the lives of those following religion in Britain today?
How might some followers of Sikhi use the gurdwara?	How might non-Sikhs use the gurdwara?
What is the context? (Sikhi focus - where is it?)	What inside a gurdwara signifies it as a place of worship?

Why are places of worship, or buildings for a community to meet in, of importance? (The gurdwara in Sikhi.)

- Who is the audience?
- What key terms are used inside? (spoken or written)
- Does a gurdwara reflect the overall message of all Sikhi followers?

Is this teaching for everyone and for all the time?	What questions do you have about the purpose of a gurdwara?

Visitors in the classroom (in-person and virtually)

Inviting visitors from different religions and also non-religious backgrounds into your primary RE lessons is essential for several reasons. It not only promotes better understanding for your pupils, but also allows for your teaching to be given context. It promotes diversity and inclusion, allowing pupils to experience a variety of worldviews and cultural practices first-hand, particularly as so many curricula focus on the threads of experience. This exposure helps young learners to appreciate the variety of beliefs and traditions that exist within their communities and beyond. It also gives them a context for their own community and surroundings and may introduce them to people with whom they have never come into contact before.

Interactions with religious visitors provide authenticity to the curriculum. Children have the space to ask questions and receive personal insights that go beyond textbook information, making the learning experience more engaging and memorable. Hearing stories and perspectives directly from practitioners helps to demystify religious practices and humanises the abstract concepts often discussed in RE classes. This is also a great way to either begin a new topic or build up to it, using the question generator to help (see page xvi).

Being exposed to a range of diverse religious visitors supports critical thinking and open-mindedness. It encourages pupils to reflect on their own beliefs and assumptions, promoting a more reflective and inquisitive mindset. By learning about different religious practices directly from those who live them, children will gain a deeper, more nuanced understanding of the diverse society in which we live.

If it is not possible to arrange an in-person visit, there is ample opportunity for a visit to happen online. A virtual visit means that your visitor can be chosen depending on your specific enquiry of learning, and the visitor can be from anywhere in the country (or world!).

There are many ways in which to organise a virtual visit:

- Request a school speaker with Humanists UK: https://humanists.uk/education/teachers/request-volunteer-school
- Request a school speaker for Islam: https://discoverislam.co.uk/schools
- Request a school speaker for evangelism: www.message.org.uk/book-a-speaker
- Contact local places of worship, such as mosques, mandirs and gurdwaras, to enquire about whether they are able to provide a speaker to visit your school.
- Contact local university religious societies to enquire about the possibility of a pupil visiting your school.

Trips to religious buildings and institutions

Trips to religious buildings and institutions are a fun and also crucial aspect of your RE teaching and the pupils' learning experience for several reasons. Firstly, these visits bring the curriculum to life, in a similar way to receiving visitors. However, with visits, pupils have the opportunity to view a religion in the real world, as opposed to in their familiar classroom setting. Seeing and experiencing the architecture, symbols and artefacts within places of worship provides a tangible connection to the concepts discussed in the classroom, making learning more engaging and memorable for your pupils.

Secondly, such trips enhance cultural and religious literacy. By visiting diverse religious sites like churches, mosques, temples and synagogues, pupils gain a deeper understanding of the practices and rituals of different faith communities. It also gives their learning a brand-new perspective and allows for a new insight into their own town or city.

These visits provide experiential learning opportunities, where children can observe religious ceremonies or practices, which can be more impactful than theoretical learning. This immersive approach helps to solidify their understanding of the significance and meaning behind various religious customs.

Visits to religious buildings enrich RE learning by providing experiential, engaging and culturally enlightening opportunities that foster respect, understanding and critical thinking among primary school pupils.

Trips not only provide a positive opportunity for pupils but they are also an excellent source of CPD for teachers.

Trips can:

- **Enhance subject knowledge:** Direct experience of religious spaces, rituals and artefacts deepens teachers' understanding of the beliefs and practices that they teach. This first-hand knowledge enriches their lessons, making them more accurate and engaging for pupils.
- **Provide pedagogical insights:** Observing how religious communities use their spaces for worship, education and social activities can offer new ideas and approaches for teaching about these religions. Teachers can learn about different ways in which to explain complex religious concepts and practices to their pupils.
- **Encourage professional networking:** Teachers can connect with religious leaders and practitioners, forming relationships that can be valuable for arranging future educational visits, guest speakers or collaborative projects. These connections can provide ongoing support and resources for teaching RE.

Finally, such visits promote reflective practice. Teachers can reflect on their own beliefs and assumptions, enhancing their ability to approach RE with an open mind. This reflection is crucial for teaching RE in a balanced and unbiased way, ensuring that all children feel respected and understood, as well as for ensuring that the curriculum is a real reflection of learning with a purpose.

Teaching Primary RE

Curriculum enrichment

Curriculum enrichment in RE is like adding sprinkles and a cherry on top of a cake – it takes something already good and makes it even more exciting and engaging! Your curriculum can engage, be fun and also hit all the learning goals for your children, while also creating connections across year groups and subjects. Imagine your usual RE lessons but supercharged with activities and events that bring everything to life.

First off, think **assemblies** that are like mini world tours. One day you're celebrating Diwali with vibrant dances and colourful rangoli; the next you're hearing tales of courage from a rabbi during Hanukkah. It's a great way in which to start the day with a cultural bang! Moreover, it allows for the children to be engaged at any stage and journey in the curriculum.

Then there are **celebrations in school**, when you get hands-on fun. Picture your school sampling sweets during Eid or decorating Easter eggs. These celebrations turn learning into a joyous experience that children look forward to, year in, year out.

Curriculum weeks are like deep-dives into the religions that your children will learn about on their journey of RE. They provide an opportunity to reimagine RE learning through an entire week where classrooms transform into different countries and cultures, each showcasing their unique religious traditions through interactive exhibits, food tastings and role-playing activities. It's like a mini festival right in your school!

And don't forget the **cross-curricular links** – where RE teams up with other subjects. Think art classes making mandalas, history lessons on ancient religious sites or geography exploring pilgrimage routes. It's all about seeing how religion connects with everything else in our world.

So, curriculum enrichment in RE? It's all about making learning as fun and vibrant as a carnival, with plenty of opportunities to explore, create and celebrate!

Assemblies

Integrating RE into school assemblies can enrich the curriculum by creating opportunities for all pupils to learn about and celebrate various religious traditions. Assemblies can feature guest speakers from different faith communities, storytelling, music and performances that highlight important religious festivals and moral teachings. This not only raises awareness but also nurtures an inclusive environment, where diverse beliefs are respected and appreciated. For example, assemblies on Diwali, Christmas, Eid and other religious holidays can provide insights into the significance and practices of these events, enhancing pupils' cultural understanding and empathy.

They can also be used as a chance for classes to share their learning from the classroom to the whole school, giving a sneak preview of what's to come for other year groups, as well as a possible revision for others.

Celebrations in school

Celebrating religious festivals and important cultural events within the school environment is another way of bringing RE to life. Schools can organise activities and events that allow pupils to actively participate in the customs and traditions of various religions. For instance, creating art projects, sharing traditional foods and participating in dances or plays related to specific religious festivals can make the learning experience interactive and engaging.

Such celebrations can be scheduled throughout the school year to ensure continuous exposure and learning about different faiths and cultures. This is where your curriculum mapping and journey are key. If one year group isn't exploring Sikhism specifically, for example, they will still be exposed to it through the commemoration of Diwali during Diwali day or week.

Curriculum weeks

Dedicated RE curriculum weeks provide an in-depth focus on specific religious themes or traditions. These thematic weeks can involve a range of activities, such as workshops, guest lectures, trips to places of worship and collaborative projects.

For example, a week focusing on 'World Religions' could include a mix of classroom activities, visits to local religious sites and interactive sessions with representatives from different faiths. This immersive approach allows pupils to explore religious concepts more deeply and gain a comprehensive understanding of the subject.

What is key with this approach is not to rely on it as your go-to for RE teaching; effective RE should be consistent. Such weeks merely enhance the learning already happening across your school.

Cross-curricular links

Linking RE with other subjects can create a more holistic and integrated learning experience. For example, RE can be connected with history to explore the historical context of religions, with geography to understand the global distribution of religious communities and with literature to study religious texts and stories.

Art and music classes can incorporate religious themes, while social studies can examine the role of religion in society. These cross-curricular links help children to see the relevance of religious education in various aspects of life and to foster critical thinking and interdisciplinary learning. Moreover, they allow for discussions with curriculum and subject leads to find links, tighten the curriculum for a seamless flow and also promote one another's subjects.

By enriching the RE curriculum through assemblies, celebrations, curriculum weeks and cross-curricular links, schools can create a vibrant and inclusive educational environment that promotes understanding, respect and appreciation for the diverse religious and cultural traditions that shape our world.

It all comes back to having impactful and excellent RE in our schools and classrooms.

Part 1

Key Stage 1

1 The disciplinary skills

As discussed in the introduction, disciplinary knowledge in RE in English primary schools refers to the skills, methods and approaches that teachers use as the underlying threads when teaching (Diocese of Lincoln Board of Education, 2021).

These particular skills will aid pupils to develop, understand, analyse and engage with religious and non-religious ideas.

Disciplinary skills involve the application of critical thinking and research skills, and the ability to evaluate information in the context of the study of religion. This book will cover how this looks in both Key Stage 1 and Key Stage 2, and will explore how we can create a harmonious journey from one key stage to the next.

Navigating the world: Religious Education in Key Stage 1

How do the disciplinary skills play out in Key Stage 1?

In the foundational stage of Key Stage 1, the disciplinary skills in RE serve as a compass, guiding young learners in their exploration of diverse belief systems.

As pupils begin to embark on this journey, guidance for teachers and curriculum creators can be obtained from multiple sources, including the recommendations set out by the Standing Advisory Council for Religious Education (SACRE) of the school's local authority. Other influences might include the National Content Standard for RE in England (Religious Education Council, 2023), as well as NATRE (National Association of Teachers of Religious Education, www.natre.org.uk/primary/re-at-primary-level).

At this stage of learning, the most important factors are developing foundational knowledge, sparking curiosity and nurturing a respectful understanding of religious diversity. Disciplinary skills start to manifest as children engage in age-appropriate activities that encourage enquiry, such as storytelling, visual exploration and guided discussions.

Within the framework of SACRE recommendations, Key Stage 1 RE activities prioritise age-appropriate questioning and exploration. Pupils are gently introduced to fundamental concepts, such as the meaning of sacred texts, places of worship and basic religious vocabulary. The goal is not to overwhelm but to lay a solid foundation for future learning.

In the table on page 3, we can see that the questions have been ordered according to the disciplinary threads 'Discover', 'Explore' and 'Connect'. Autonomy is, of course, important when planning your schemes of work, but knowing that a certain question feeds well into a specific thread is useful. The recommendations available via the SACRE-suggested units of work aid in this; schools have access to their local agreed syllabus online through their local authority sites. Slight deviation or manipulation of the questions is possible, and whether or not to do this will depend on the experience of the teachers organising and planning the curriculum units, but having pre-determined questions as a reference point is useful. In this table, it is possible to see the progression in questioning from Foundation Stage leading into Key Stage 1, and how this feeds and supplements what the pupils will eventually reach at lower Key Stage 2. Chronological progression is key.

Foundation Stage	**Discover**	Which stories are special to some people? Why?
Key Stage 1	**Explore**	What is Christianity? What do Christians believe? What is Judaism? What do Jews believe? What is Islam? What do Muslims believe?
Lower Key Stage 2	**Connect**	What are different beliefs about God?

As a reminder, here is the list from the Introduction of disciplinary threads in RE, which are particular to the school's curriculum outline, but may include the following.

1. **Critical thinking:** Encouraging pupils to think critically about religious and ethical questions, enabling them to evaluate different perspectives and develop their own reasoned opinions. This can sometimes come under the SACRE-suggested threads of 'exploring' and 'connecting'.

2. **Analytical skills:** Helping pupils to analyse religious texts, rituals and practices, considering their historical, cultural and social contexts. Making connections between different religions and worldviews while also understanding their own rituals.

3. **Reflection and Expression:** Encouraging pupils to reflect on their own beliefs and values, as well as providing opportunities for them to express their thoughts and opinions on religious and ethical matters.

4. **Respectful dialogue:** Promoting respectful and open dialogue about religious and non-religious perspectives, fostering an understanding of diverse viewpoints and expressing this in a respectful manner.

These should fall in line with (although not necessarily mirror) the idea of the three strands suggested by SACREs, in conjunction with RE Today (n.d.), of 'Believing', 'Expressing' and 'Living'. These disciplinary threads will help to ensure that Key Stage 1 pupils have the foundational knowledge to question, reflect and express, before attempting larger or more complex questions and subject knowledge.

> **Tip:** *Have your disciplinary skills presented on all walls of work, displays and lesson slides or sheets, to familiarise pupils with the concepts and their usage.*

RELIGIOUS CELEBRATION
Fire exit

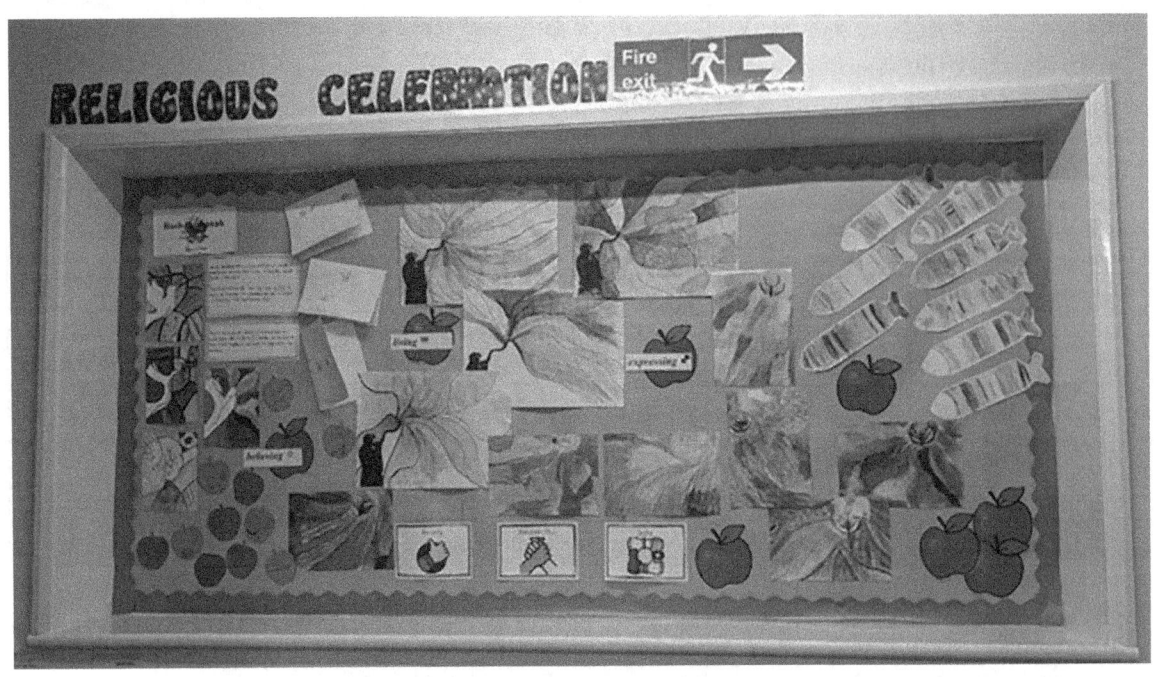

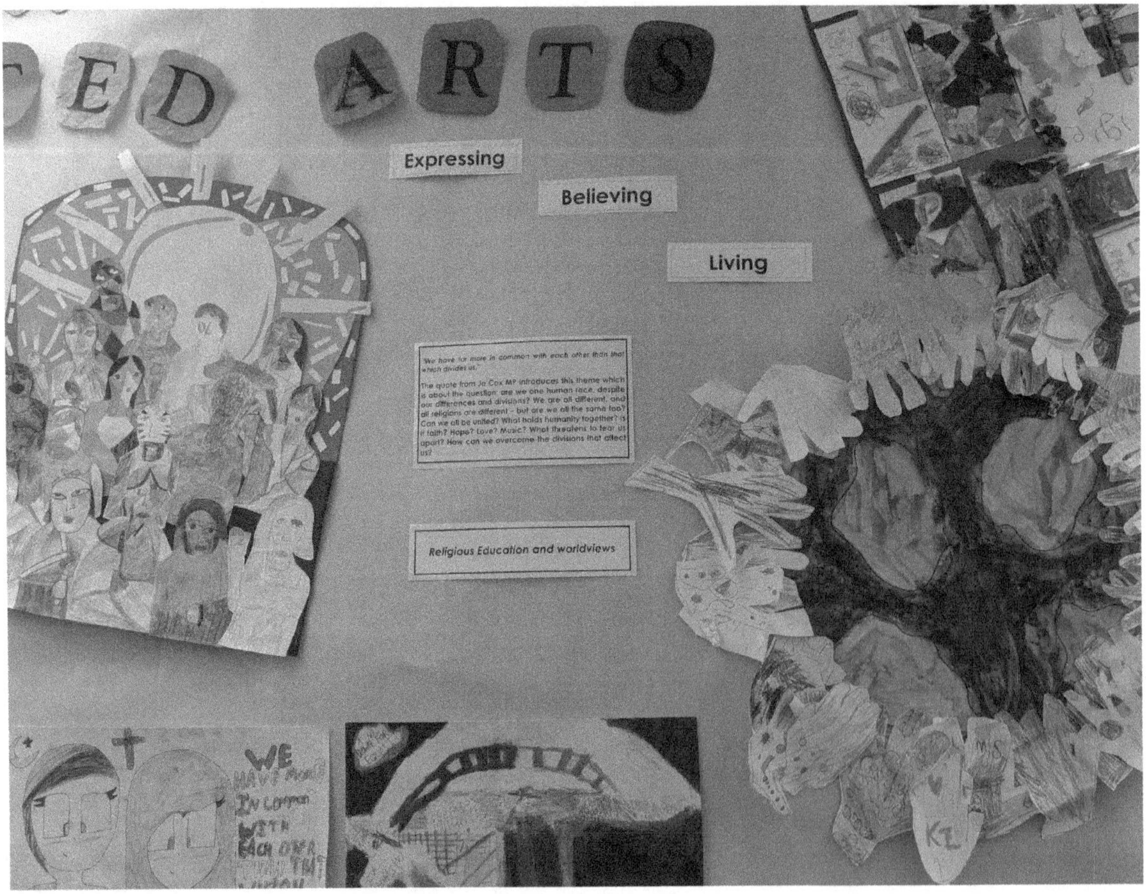
ED ARTS
Expressing
Believing
Living
"We have far more in common with each other than that which divides us."
The quote from Jo Cox MP introduces this theme which is about the question: are we one human race, despite our differences and divisions? We are all different, and all religions are different – but are we all the same too? Can we all be united? What holds humanity together? Is it faith? Hope? Love? Music? What threatens to tear us apart? How can we overcome the divisions that affect us?
Religious Education and worldviews

2 Substantive knowledge: The Abrahamic faiths

What do I need to know?

The introduction to the Abrahamic faiths in Key Stage 1 builds the foundation for children's learning through the disciplinary threads and allows for better interconnected understanding between the three Abrahamic faiths to create those crucial links.

Figure 2.1 offers a basic overview of the links between the three Abrahamic faiths and provides key pieces of information that will aid your teaching for better accuracy. The infographic will also translate well from year group to year group.

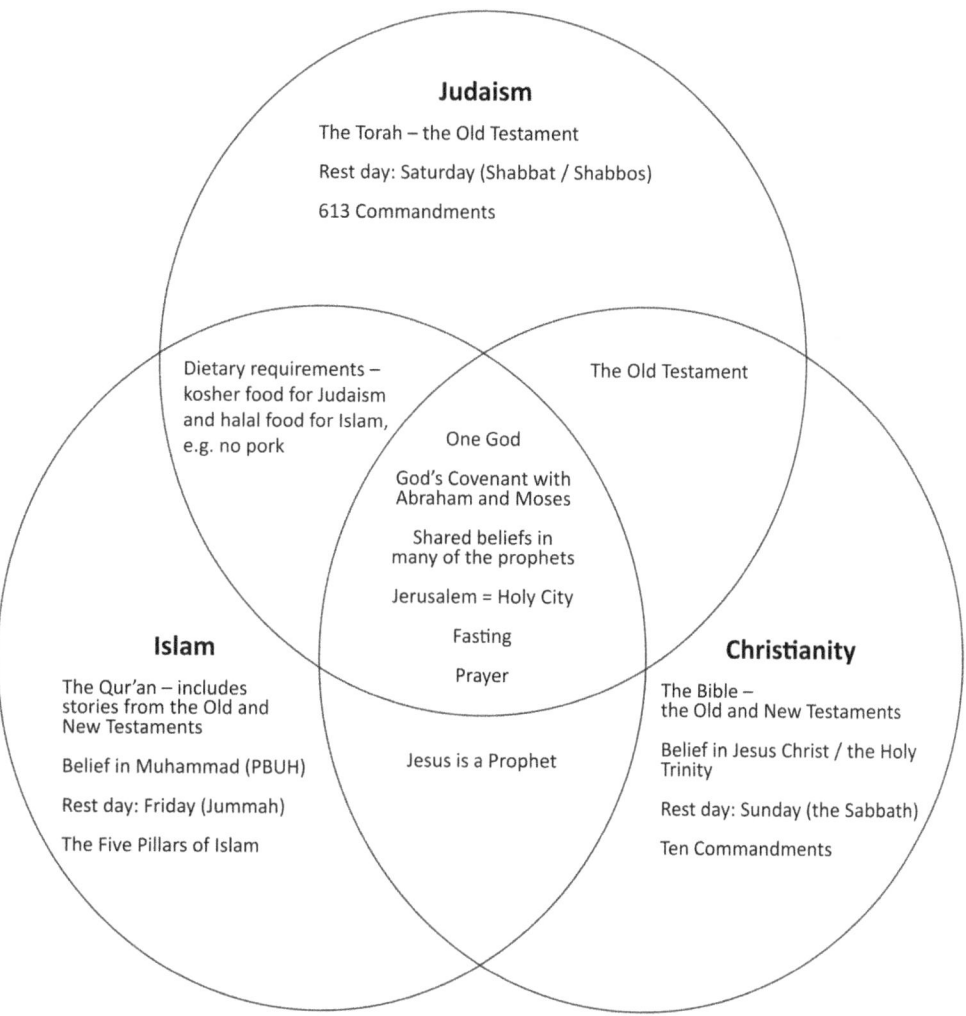

FIGURE 2.1: The links between the three Abrahamic faiths

Quick vocab check

Abrahamic: a group of three major religions – Judaism, Christianity and Islam – whose spiritual lineage can be traced back to the biblical figure Abraham. These religions share common historical and religious roots.

Religion: a set of beliefs, practices and values centred around the existence of a higher power or powers. It often includes moral and ethical guidelines for how people should live their lives.

Faith: a strong belief in something, especially without the need for proof or evidence. In a religious context, faith involves a deep trust and belief in the teachings and principles of a particular religion.

Practice: the actions, customs and behaviours associated with a particular religion. It involves how people express their beliefs in their daily lives.

Ritual: a formal and often repetitive set of actions, ceremonies or behaviours performed as part of religious worship or observance. Rituals are symbolic and have special significance within a religious community.

3 Judaism

What do I need to know?

In the foundational stages of the Key Stage 1 curriculum, children should be introduced to the fundamental tenets of Judaism. A monotheistic faith, Judaism is characterised by its distinctive rituals and key figures. These will be better understood by pupils through the use of images, videos, real-life interactions and experiences.

If we revert to the example of substantive questioning under particular disciplinary strands from the earlier SACRE, we can see that Judaism is suggested as an 'or' option for Key Stage 1. Base your choices on a number of factors, including the demographics of your school community, links to learning post-Key Stage 1 and whether you are able to make sure, as a whole-curriculum design, that Judaism will be factored in through other opportunities, such as whole-school festival commemorations.

Quick vocab check

Judaism: one of the world's oldest monotheistic religions. Judaism is the religious tradition of the Jewish people, and it encompasses their beliefs, practices and values. Central to Judaism is the worship of one God and adherence to the teachings found in the sacred texts, particularly the Torah.

Jewish: an adjective used to describe anything related to Judaism or the Jewish people. For example, Jewish traditions, culture, holidays and individuals who follow the faith are all described as 'Jewish'.

Jew: a noun used to refer to a person who practises Judaism, follows the Jewish faith and/or is part of the Jewish ethnic or religious group. Jews share a common heritage, culture and history, and they are found in various parts of the world. It's important to note that being Jewish can be both a religious and cultural identity.

Monotheistic: relating to the belief that there is only one God.

Torah: the central text of Judaism, containing the first five books of the Hebrew Bible, outlining laws and teachings.

Shabbat candles: candles lit on Friday evening to welcome Shabbat, symbolising peace and the transition into the day of rest.

Sabbath (Shabbat): the Jewish day of rest, from Friday evening to Saturday evening, dedicated to worship, rest and family time. Shabbat is also the Hebrew word for Saturday and the Sabbath.

Rabbi: a Jewish religious leader and teacher, often responsible for leading services, offering spiritual guidance and teaching the Torah.

Synagogue: Jewish places of worship and community gathering, where services, prayers and educational activities take place.

Kosher: foods prepared and consumed according to Jewish dietary laws, regulating what is permissible to eat and how it is prepared.

Hanukkah: Jewish festival lasting eight days, celebrating the rededication of the Second Temple, marked by lighting menorah candles.

Passover: Jewish holiday commemorating the Israelites' Exodus from Egypt, celebrated with a special meal (Seder) and symbolic foods.

Rituals

Rituals play a central role in Jewish practice. Pupils should learn about the lighting of Shabbat candles – a tradition marking the beginning of the Sabbath – by the end of Key Stage 1. They should understand the significance of synagogues as places of worship, where the veneration of the Torah takes precedence. Basic facts include the recognition of the Star of David, which is a symbol representing unity within the Jewish faith. These are all important for the foundations in Key Stage 1. Pupils should also be acquainted with kosher dietary practices and engage in the observance of festivals such as Hanukkah and Passover.

Key figures

Pupils should be introduced to the rabbi, a living example of a Jewish leader in the community, as the person employed by the synagogue to lead worship and provide spiritual guidance. In addition to this, key characters from the story of Hanukkah, such as the Maccabees, and figures such as Moses and Pharoah in the story of Passover should be introduced.

A rabbi can be described to pupils as a special teacher in the Jewish community. They help people to understand and follow the teachings of Judaism. Rabbis lead prayers, teach about the Torah (the holy book) and provide guidance. They are helpers who answer questions and support families. Rabbis make the community feel connected and cared for.

Useful links:

www.bbc.co.uk/bitesize/topics/zqbw2hv/articles/zvwphcw

www.bbc.co.uk/bitesize/articles/z737dp3

Crafting

Pupils should actively participate in crafting symbolic items, such as menorahs for Hanukkah, which promotes a hands-on approach to learning and a link to their learning in the Early Years Foundation Stage. The preparation of challah bread, for example, serves as a tactile means of comprehending the sanctity associated with Shabbat. Additionally, exposure to Jewish festivals through basic artistic expression further enriches the learning experience.

Useful links:

www.natre.org.uk/resources/year-1-who-is-jewish-and-how-do-they-live-ko

https://classroom.thenational.academy/lessons/how-do-jews-express-their-faith-today-6ou6at

Lesson 1: What does it mean to be Jewish?

Disciplinary: beliefs and rituals

You will need
- paper
- pens and pencils
- pictures of diverse children and families
- pictures of synagogues and pictures or objects depicting the Star of David and menorahs
- video content about life as a follower of Judaism, such as: www.bbc.co.uk/teach/class-clips-video/religious-studies-ks2-what-is-judaism/zfbhf4j
- Jewish Museum London – 'A family's home': https://jewishmuseum.org.uk/schools/asset/a-familys-home

Getting started

Begin the lesson by introducing the concept of different beliefs and cultures. Show images of diverse children and families, explaining that people around the world have various backgrounds and beliefs. Establish a basic understanding that everyone is unique and that we all celebrate different occasions in different ways.

Keep it simple and engaging, asking questions like 'Can anyone name an event that people celebrate?' and 'What do you celebrate with your family?'.

Explain to the children that they will be learning about the Jewish community and what they believe. Use visuals or object-handling of a menorah and a Star of David, both symbols of Judaism, to spark curiosity.

Class activities

1. Play a game where children take turns sharing something special from their own families, reinforcing the idea that everyone's beliefs are important. Encourage questions and curiosity throughout the activity. This could be a sharing game, where children sit in a circle and share but only the person holding an item is allowed to speak. When they have shared, they then pass the item onto the next person.
2. Read or watch a short, age-appropriate story about a Jewish family, emphasising their customs and beliefs.
3. Show pictures of a synagogue and explain its significance – for example, the names of each section of the synagogue, where the Torah is kept, and where worshippers sit or stand.
4. Introduce basic Jewish terms like 'Shabbat' and 'Torah', associating them with positive experiences. This can be done through watching videos of followers of Judaism partaking in rituals that include the Torah, in the synagogue or at home.

Plenary material

Conclude the lesson by revisiting the initial question: Who is Jewish and what do they believe? This will be a question that you keep revisiting during the journey of learning.

Recap key points about Jewish beliefs, symbols and practices; this can be done by playing the game outlined above.

Use a short video that reinforces the lesson's concepts in a fun and memorable way. This will prepare pupils for the next session, to review before building new knowledge. The Jewish Museum in London has videos of real-life Jewish families here: https://jewishmuseum.org.uk/schools/asset/a-familys-shabbat

Recording of learning

Recording of learning can be through photographs in books or displays, as well as a floorbook to review with the class in the next lesson. Floorbooks are an opportunity to showcase the class's learning in one shared A2-size book, where all notes, photos and discussions can be recorded and displayed in class.

Lesson 2: Jewish symbols and the importance in Jewish practice

Disciplinary: beliefs and rituals

You will need
- For effective object-handling, physical objects such as a menorah, photos of synagogues and a Torah are useful.
- An item that allows for only the child holding the item to talk, to encourage listening to others when discussing.
- The story of Hanukkah for Key Stage 1: www.bbc.co.uk/teach/class-clips-video/religious-studies-ks1-the-jewish-story-of-hanukkah/z47wxyc or a similar resource

Getting started

Begin the lesson by revisiting the last lesson's concept of different beliefs and cultures. This is a good time for children to reflect on their own beliefs once more, as well as the different beliefs of other children in the class.

Revisit the visual and/or object-handling of a menorah, a symbol of Judaism, to engage conversation and discussion. This time, focus on the key vocabulary (see pages 7–8) to establish a basic understanding of this symbol.

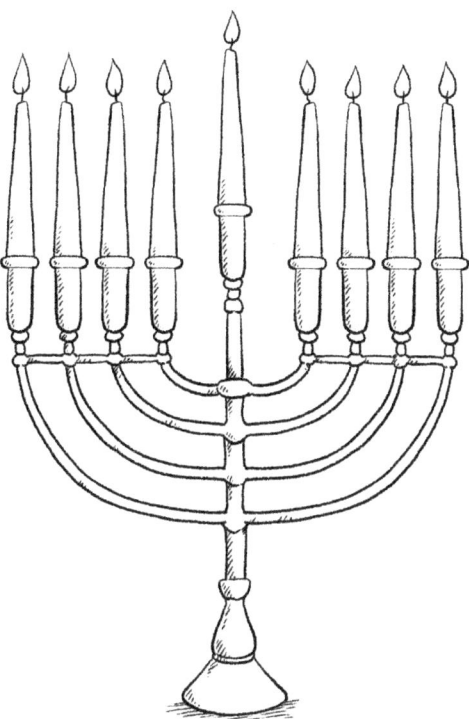

Explain that a menorah is a special candle holder with nine branches. Jewish people light it during Hanukkah to celebrate a miracle. Each night, they add a new candle, using the middle one, called the 'shamash', to light the others. It's a joyful symbol of hope and faith.

This activity can be repeated with other Jewish symbols and objects, such as the kippah, Torah or a dreidel (see page 13 for more detail). For example, children can explore the use of a kippah and then discuss the name of the object, its use and its significance, through class discussion.

Class activities
1. Read or watch an age-appropriate retelling of the story of Hanukkah. Are children able to place the symbol of the menorah in this story?
2. Revise Jewish vocabulary, like 'menorah' and 'Torah', associating them with the story of Hanukkah. Children can discuss the importance of the Torah and its role. Can they recognise the various objects and symbols discussed in the context of the story?

Plenary material
Conclude the lesson by asking the children, 'Which important symbols can you identify related to Judaism?' The children should be able to refer to the various symbols and the story from their learning.

Revisit the initial question from Lesson 1, 'Who is Jewish and what do they believe?', to encourage discussion of the story of Hanukkah and why it is celebrated. This will be a question that you keep revisiting during the journey of learning.

Recording of learning
Recording of learning can be through photographs in books or displays, as well as a floorbook, to review with the class in the next lesson. This can lead on from the previous lesson, to show a journey of learning in the class floorbook.

Useful links:
www.bbc.co.uk/teach/class-clips-video/religious-studies-ks1-the-jewish-story-of-hanukkah/z47wxyc

Lesson 3: Judaism in the home
Disciplinary: beliefs and rituals

You will need
- physical objects such as a menorah, dreidel and kippah for object-handling
- paper and pens.

Judaism

Getting started

Begin the lesson by revisiting the Jewish symbols discussed in Lesson 2. Are children able to relate these to the story of Hanukkah? For example, a menorah and why it is used during the festival.

Revisit the visual and/or object-handling of a menorah, a symbol of Judaism, to engage conversation and discussion. Rewatch or retell the story of Hanukkah as a class. This will reactivate the children's prior knowledge in order to build on this lesson.

Explore the use of the menorah at home, with an introduction to other Jewish symbols and objects also used during Hanukkah. Children could have the opportunity to handle a kippah and/or dreidel, further exploring what may be in a Jewish home. A kippah (also known as a yarmulke) is a small, rounded cap worn by Jewish men and sometimes women, as a sign of reverence and respect for God. A dreidel is a spinning top used during the Jewish holiday of Hanukkah in a traditional game. It has four sides, each marked with a Hebrew letter: nun, gimel, hei and shin, which stand for 'A great miracle happened there' (referring to the Hanukkah miracle of the oil).

Children will be able to build their learning to gain an understanding of what Jewish life at home may look like for some followers of Judaism.

Class activities

1. Reflect on how Jewish people find blessing in the story of Hanukkah and revisit the idea of how different people celebrate different things at home.
2. Enquiry questions to consider: How do Jewish people celebrate Hanukkah at home? How might this look? Encourage pupils to use the correct vocabulary (see page 3).
3. Draw a picture of a Hanukkah celebration at home, labelling the different elements used during the festival. Children can present this to one another in class.

Plenary material

Conclude the lesson by asking the question, 'How is Hanukkah celebrated at home for Jewish people?' Discuss as a class.

Recording of learning

Create a class one-pager, display or class assembly to showcase the learning. A one-pager is an elevated version of a poster that is a mixture of facts and pictures, drawn by the pupils on one page (either A4 or in their books) and encompassing the lesson's learning.

Lesson 4: Celebrating Hanukkah through food

Disciplinary: beliefs and rituals

You will need
- the story of Hanukkah for Key Stage 1: www.bbc.co.uk/teach/class-clips-video/religious-studies-ks1-the-jewish-story-of-hanukkah/z47wxyc
- ingredients to make latkes:
  - 3 medium-sized potatoes, peeled
  - 1 large egg, beaten
  - 2 tbsp plain flour
  - 1 tbsp grated onion
  - ¼ tsp salt
  - oil for shallow frying
  - a large bowl
  - a wooden spoon
  - a frying pan
  - a heat-proof spatula
  - a heat source for frying.

Safety warning: Always check for food allergies before the lesson.

Getting started

Revise the story of Hanukkah with the class by showing them the video. Can the pupils remember the story from their previous lessons?

Through the revision of the Hanukkah story, children can then explore its traditions by making latkes, a traditional food made and eaten by Jewish people during this festival. Through this, pupils will learn about the significance of oil in Hanukkah and explore the idea of celebration and community.

As reiterated in the story, explain that Hanukkah is a Jewish holiday celebrated for eight nights. It commemorates a miracle that happened long ago, when a small amount of oil kept a lamp burning for eight days in a sacred temple. Show pupils a picture of a menorah and remind pupils of its significance in the Hanukkah celebration.

Explain that one way in which Jewish families celebrate Hanukkah is by eating foods cooked in oil, like latkes, to remember the miracle of the oil.

Preparing to make latkes:
1. Show the class the ingredients needed for the latkes.
2. Prepare the latkes by mixing together the potatoes, onion, egg, flour and salt in a bowl. Invite the pupils to help by adding the ingredients to the bowl and stirring the ingredients together.
3. In a safe cooking setup, heat oil in a frying pan over a medium-high heat; you need quite a lot of oil, so that the oil is around 1cm deep in the pan. Place large spoonfuls of the mixture into the hot oil, pressing down on them to form patties.
4. Cook for around four to five minutes until golden brown. Flip and cook for another four to five minutes.

Explain to the children that cooking in oil reminds Jewish people of the oil that lasted eight days. While cooking, discuss how food can be a part of traditions and celebrations. Ask questions such as 'Why do you think that food is important in celebrations?' and 'What foods do you eat during special times?'.

Plenary material
After the latkes have cooled, invite the pupils to taste them. Encourage them to talk about the flavours and how they feel about making something from a different tradition. Conclude with a brief reflection on how food can bring people together, help us to celebrate and remind us of important stories or traditions.

Recording of learning
Recording of learning can be through photographs in books or displays, as well as a floorbook to review with the class in the next lesson. This can lead on from the previous lesson.

Useful links:
www.bbc.co.uk/teach/class-clips-video/religious-studies-ks1-the-jewish-story-of-hanukkah/z47wxyc

Lesson 5: Key Jewish figures – the story of Moses

Disciplinary: beliefs

You will need
- story of Moses video: www.bbc.co.uk/teach/class-clips-video/articles/zmfp382
- story of Moses book – *Moses and the Exodus Express* by Paul Kerensa
- paper and colouring pens
- sand
- rocks
- small-world figures.

Getting started

Begin the lesson by discussing with the pupils who the important people are in their lives. These could be parents and carers, teachers and/or people in the community. Why are they important?

This will be a prompt to introduce the pupils to the figure of Moses in Judaism.

In Judaism, Moses is a very special leader, chosen by God to help the Jewish people. A long time ago, the Jewish people were slaves in Egypt and they were treated very badly. God asked Moses to tell the king, called Pharaoh, to let the people go. After Pharaoh said 'no' many times, God sent ten plagues to show His power. Finally, Pharaoh agreed, and Moses led the Jewish people out of Egypt to freedom. Moses also climbed a big mountain, where God gave him the Ten Commandments – special rules to help people to live good lives.

Some key questions to consider during the lesson are:

- Who was Moses? (This encourages pupils to recall who he is in the story.)
- What did Moses help the Jewish people to do? (This prompts pupils to think about the Exodus from Egypt.)
- What are the Ten Commandments? (This introduces pupils to the idea of rules given by God.)
- Why did God choose Moses? (This encourages discussion about leadership and faith.)
- What lessons can we learn from Moses? (This encourages pupils to think about kindness, bravery and following rules.)

Class activities
1. Reflect on how Jewish people see Moses as a leader and create a character board of Moses as a class or in pairs. What adjectives can be used to describe Moses?
2. **Moses in the desert activity:** Set up a sensory play area with sand, rocks and toy figures to recreate the scene of the Israelites in the desert. Encourage children to play out scenes from Moses's journey, discussing how the people followed him.
3. **Role-playing activity:** Organise a simple role-play, where children can act out parts of Moses' story, such as leading the Israelites or talking to Pharaoh. Discuss feelings and challenges that Moses might have faced.

Plenary material
Conclude the lesson by asking the question 'What makes a good leader?' and rewatch or reread the story of Moses.

Recording of learning
Record the children's role-plays and reflections to either be shown on a school portal or saved on your school system. Photos can be taken of any work done and stuck in appropriate learning books.

4 Christianity

What do I need to know?

In the foundational stages of the Key Stage 1 curriculum, children should be introduced to the fundamental tenets of Christianity. A monotheistic faith, Christians believe in one God and follow the teachings of Jesus Christ from the Bible.

Christianity is a belief system centred on Jesus Christ. Christians believe in love and kindness, and that Jesus is the Son of God.

These ideas of love and kindness, through the teachings of Jesus Christ, will be best understood by your pupils through images, videos, real-life interactions and experiences.

Quick vocab check

Christianity: a monotheistic religion based on the life and teachings of Jesus Christ. It emphasises faith, love and salvation and is rooted in the belief in the Holy Trinity – Father, Son and Holy Spirit. The Bible serves as the sacred scripture, guiding Christian beliefs and practices.

Christian: an adherent of Christianity, and someone who follows the teachings of Jesus Christ. Christians believe in the divinity of Jesus, salvation through faith and living by moral and ethical principles outlined in the Bible.

Jesus Christ: the central figure in Christianity, believed by Christians to be the Son of God and the Saviour. His teachings on love, compassion and salvation form the basis of Christian rules. The crucifixion and resurrection of Jesus are pivotal events in Christian theology, and are further explored through festivals and celebrations in Key Stages 1 and 2 (see pages 21 and 53).

Vocabulary breakdown:

CHRIST (root or prefix)
Christ refers to Jesus, believed to be the Saviour and the Son of God.

Christ – mas

The word 'Christmas' comes from the combination of the words 'Christ' and 'mass'. The term 'Christmas' is used to refer to the church festival observed annually in memory of the birth of Christ.

Christ – ened

This is when a person, often a baby, is officially named in a religious ceremony, like baptism.

Rituals and practices

Christianity's main rituals are introduced at Key Stage 1 through the festivals and practices of Christians, whether through enactment of these rituals in school (context-dependent) or planned through festivals in the curriculum.

Central among these is the act of baptism, a symbolic cleansing ritual marking entry into the Christian community. Pupils could learn about the significance of the Holy Communion, a sacred ceremony commemorating the Last Supper, where Christians partake in bread and wine to symbolise Christ's sacrifice. Key Stage 1 activities may involve simple role-playing exercises that elucidate these rituals, fostering an experiential grasp of their importance.

Other examples of rituals will include the rituals of worship and what this may look like – for example, through hymns and song, reading the Bible and listening to sermons.

Symbols

When exploring Christianity, symbols should be explored through both imagery and object-handling, so that pupils have a rounded and real-life experience of what is important in Christianity.

Children should be introduced to key Christian symbols, such as the crucifix (cross) – which is emblematic of Christ's crucifixion – in order to foster an early visual literacy of religious symbolism. Other symbols to consider are the dove (representative of the Holy Spirit) and the ichthys fish symbol (a sign often used to show an affiliation with Christianity).

A key symbol in Christianity is the Bible, which is divided into the Old and New Testaments. When introducing this in Key Stage 1, it's best to be as concise but also age-friendly as possible.

Old Testament: The Old Testament is like the first part of a big storybook. It tells us about God creating the world, important people like Adam, Noah and Moses, and many stories about God's promises to the Jewish people.

New Testament: The New Testament is the second part of the storybook. It tells us about Jesus, who is very important for Christians. It shares His teachings, the good things that He did, and how He showed people how to love and be kind to one another.

Key points to consider when teaching:

Old Testament: Stories about creation and the Jewish people.

New Testament: Stories about Jesus and His teachings.

Teaching Primary RE

Key figures

In Christianity, foremost among the key figures is Jesus Christ, whose life and teachings – including pivotal events like the Nativity and the Resurrection – are foundational to Christian doctrine. Pupils should also be introduced to figures such as Mary and Joseph, gaining insight into their roles within the Christian narrative. Age-appropriate storytelling aids can be used to weave these figures into a comprehensible tapestry, establishing a connection between the historical and religious aspects of the faith – for example, using maps to locate where the stories of Jesus Christ occurred, and timelines of when events happened during his lifetime.

Pupils should also be given the opportunity to understand figures of Christianity within a community context, such as priests and youth pastors. Priests can be described to pupils as being religious leaders who perform ceremonies and prayers and provide guidance.

Useful links:

www.bbc.co.uk/bitesize/topics/zdykjxs/articles/zpk6xbk

Crafting

Children should actively participate in crafting symbolic and simple baptismal symbols or engaging in communal 'feasts' to understand the significance of Holy Communion and Harvest. Storytelling, reinforced by visual aids, serves as a channel for exploring the lives of key figures, fostering an interactive and dynamic learning environment. Links to the local community and Churches are also recommended in order to encourage a deeper understanding of the faith.

Useful links:

www.natre.org.uk/uploads/Free%20Resources/Christianity%20Stewardship%20KS1%20.pdf

https://classroom.thenational.academy/lessons/what-might-christians-do-at-church-at-christmas-6otk2d?from_query=christianity+key+stage+1

If we revert to the example of substantive questioning under particular disciplinary strands from the earlier SACRE, we can see that Christianity is suggested as a key option throughout Key Stage 1, leading all the way into Key Stage 4.

According to the Education Act of 1996, local authorities require that the syllabus reflects the religious traditions of Great Britain, which are in the main instance Christian, while taking account of the teaching and practices of the other principal religions represented in Great Britain.

Lesson 1: – Exploring Christianity and what makes Christians feel special

Disciplinary: beliefs and rituals

You will need
- items for object-handling, including rosary beads and a crucifix
- paper and coloured pencils
- storybooks relating to Christianity, such as *Children's Bible Stories* (Autumn Publishing)
- the story book *Take and Eat: Bible Stories for Kids about the Eucharist* (by Jared Dees)
- a video showing a baptism, such as: www.bbc.co.uk/teach/class-clips-video/articles/zm32nrdKS2
- an item of importance for the teacher/other adults working in the classroom – perhaps a shared item that is special to the class, e.g. a class mascot.

Getting started:

Begin the lesson by introducing the concept of feeling special. Ask the children questions such as, 'How do you feel special?' and 'Is there a specific event that makes you feel special?'.

List all of the events in and out of school that can make one feel special. This would be a perfect opportunity to showcase what is special to the teacher to the class, and explain why it is special. It could be a photo, an item of clothing or a religious item particularly special to the teacher. This lays a foundation to the pupils of what is deemed special and why.

Use visuals or object-handling of, for example, school certificates, gift boxes and birthday cards. Include within this a crucifix and rosary beads for the children to explore.

Class activities:

These can be split into two or three lessons, in order for children to learn varying ideas of Christian experiences. The sequence of lessons can be used to show progression and also to cement the overall objective for the pupils in different ways.

1. **Lesson 1:** Read age-appropriate picture books or stories that showcase characters experiencing special moments in a Christian context, such as a Holy Communion. Discuss how these characters feel special in the stories. Has anyone in the class experienced something similar? Create a board with children's ideas about how the characters feel special.

2. **Lesson 2:** Watch a video on a Christian event, such as a baptism, and discuss why Christians may choose to be baptised and why this is special. Create a board with ideas about why this is a special event for those involved. This can then be compared to the characters in the story from a previous lesson.

3. **Lesson 3:** Play a game where children take turns sharing something special from their own families; these could be things such as a family photo, a pet or a meal that their family shares on a specific day. Encourage questions and curiosity throughout the activities, reinforcing the idea that everyone's beliefs are important. The teacher is encouraged to share something of importance for them, as an example to the children. This also lends itself as a piece of work that can be extended into home learning.

Plenary Material:

Conclude the lesson by revisiting the question, 'How do we feel special?'.

Focus on the children's own personal experiences of what makes them feel special, and explore whether any children are able to make links to Christian rituals.

Recording of learning
Children can record their work through photographs in books or displays, as well as a floor book to review with the class in the next lesson.

Useful links:
https://www.bbc.co.uk/bitesize/topics/zdykjxs/articles/ztgqjsg

https://www.natre.org.uk/resources/year-1-how-should-we-care-for-others-and-the-world-and-why-does-it-matter-ko

Lesson 2: Which Christian symbols appear in the story of Easter?

Disciplinary: beliefs and rituals

You will need
- objects to handle, such as a selection of crucifixes, or photos of crucifixes if preferred
- a story about Easter, such as: www.bbc.co.uk/teach/class-clips-video/ks1-religious-studies-the-christian-story-of-easter/zhgv47h

Getting started
Begin the lesson by revisiting the last lesson's concept of feeling special. Ask the children to name different moments in their lives where they remember feeling special. This is a good time for children to reflect on their own beliefs once more, and the differences between their beliefs and other children's.

Revisit the visuals and/or object-handling of a crucifix to engage conversation and discussion. This time, focus on the key vocabulary (see page 50) to establish a basic understanding of the symbol and its meaning. This would be an appropriate time to explore the story of Easter.

Explain that the crucifix is an important Christian symbol representing the crucifixion of Jesus Christ. It features a cross with an image or figure of Jesus, reminding believers of his sacrifice for humanity.

Crucifixion is a historical event where Jesus was nailed to a cross – a significant part of Christian beliefs. (This definition can be further explored in Key Stage 2; see page 53.)

Class activities
1. Accurately label a crucifix to match the physical object in the class. This can be a part of exploring the different objects found inside a church.

Teaching Primary RE

2. Introduce vocabulary like 'church', 'Bible' and 'heaven', associating them with the story of Easter.
3. Watch or retell the story of Easter to the class, and then ask them to map this out in a cartoon strip in their books. If preferred, the story can be retold through role-play, where children play different roles from the story of Easter. These roles should include Jesus, Mary and the disciples.

Plenary material

Recap key points about Christian beliefs from the story of Easter. Ask the children to name key symbols from their learning. Children should be able to recognise the importance of the crucifix.

Reiterate that even though the story talks about the death of Jesus, it was spreading the good news that he was OK and had gone to heaven, which made his followers feel special and reassured.

Recording of learning

Recording of learning can be through photographs of the freeze-frames from the role-play, which could then be stuck in books or displays, as well as a floorbook to review with the class in the next lesson.

Lesson 3: Why is the crucifix an important Christian symbol?

Disciplinary: beliefs

You will need

- photos of crucifixes or physical crucifixes for children to handle
- paper, card and colouring pencils
- a story of Easter to watch and explore, such as: www.bbc.co.uk/teach/class-clips-video/ks1-religious-studies-the-christian-story-of-easter/zhgv47h

Getting started

This lesson is suggested as a follow-on from Lesson 2, 'Which Christian symbols appear in the story of Easter?'.

Revisit the story of Easter, either by watching a video or by retelling the story. Ask the children questions such as 'Can you remember the name of the cross?' and 'Why is the cross important?'.

Class activities

1. Invite the children to create their own crucifixes. These can form part of an Easter commemoration or celebration (school context dependent).
2. Children can use the object-handling sessions and videos to inform their design.

Plenary material

Conclude the lesson by revisiting the question 'Why is the crucifix an important symbol?'. Their crucifixes can be used to form a display and will increase their understanding of this important Christian symbol.

Recording of learning

Present the crucifixes during an Easter assembly and around school. Photos of the crucifixes can be added to the children's RE books.

Lesson 4: What can we learn from parables?

Disciplinary: beliefs

You will need

- a parable to focus on, such as that of the lost coin: www.bbc.co.uk/teach/school-radio/articles/zxvd7v4
- a cardboard crown-shape as a base
- gold card cut into circles (large enough to write on)
- glue.

Getting started

Begin the lesson by asking the children to think about their favourite stories. Why are those stories their favourites?

Introduce children to the idea of parables. Explain to the children that a parable is a simple story that teaches an important lesson or message. It's like a special story with a hidden meaning, that helps us to understand good values and choices.

Watch or read the Parable of the Lost Coin. Can the children identify why this story is important for Christians?

Class activities

1. The Parable of the Lost Coin teaches that God is loving and looks out for everyone, so Christians in return want to show that they love God. As a class, think of some of the ways in which Christians might do this (referring back to earlier learning, such as going to church, celebrating Easter and so on).

Teaching Primary RE

2. Create a class crown with coins, representing each child and what special attributes they bring to the class. Give each child a gold circle of card and ask them to think about and write on the card what makes them special – for example, 'caring', 'loving', 'fun'. Stick the gold coins onto the crown and display.
3. Invite the children to retell the story of the Lost Coin through drama in small groups. Freeze-frame photos can be taken to be stuck in the pupils' books to showcase their learning, as well as the sequencing of the story.

Plenary material
Conclude the lesson by revisiting the question 'What can we learn from the Parable of the Lost Coin?'. Explore the idea that God is like a caregiver, helping us no matter what.

Recording of learning
Create a class one-pager, display or class assembly to showcase the pupils' learning.

Lesson 5: Who is important in the Christian community?

Disciplinary: beliefs, explore

You will need
- a question generator
- contacts with a local church to arrange a visit from a priest (this can be done virtually if an in-person visit is not an option).

Getting started
Begin the lesson by asking the children to think about who is important in their school community. Can children name all the different people in school, their role and how they help?

Next, explore the purpose of a church and who leads in a church. Explain to the children that, in school, we have a headteacher who leads the school. A priest can be likened to this in the church.

Explain to the children that a priest in Christianity is like a special helper who leads prayers, teaches about God and helps people to learn about their faith. They wear special clothes and work in churches. Priests also perform ceremonies like weddings and baptisms, and they offer support and guidance to people who need it.

Class activities

1. Fill in a question generator with appropriate questions, such as 'What is the name of the stand in the church?', in preparation for the visit from a local priest. This can be done as a whole-class input or individually in each child's book. The questions should encourage pupils to explore further the roles of important figures in Christianity, such as the priest, and why their surroundings, such as the church, are important. The question grid will help children to compartmentalise their thought processes and execute higher-level questioning.
2. During the visit, give pupils the opportunity to ask their questions. As well as answering their questions, this visit will introduce a real-life element to pupils' learning.

Plenary material

Ask the children whether they now have even more questions following the meet and greet. Encourage them to record any additional questions in their books to save for further lessons or home learning.

Revisit the role of a priest and what they do for the Christian community.

Recording of learning

Question generators can be stuck into children's books to act as a reference.

Question Generator

The question generator allows children to expand their questioning skills. This is a tool that can be used across humanities subjects and helps pupils to think beyond the basic question format.

The generator can be tailored for either key stage and additional columns can be added or taken away.

	is	*does*	*should*
What	What is the name of the cross in Christianity?		
When			
Who			
Where			Where should a Christian pray?
Why			

5 Islam

What do I need to know?

In the foundational stages of the Key Stage 1 curriculum, children should be introduced to the fundamental tenets of Islam. Completing the study of the three Abrahamic faiths, Islam should be introduced to children through their learning, as well as real-life experiences and whole-school commemorations.

Introducing Islam into the Key Stage 1 curriculum is essential for fostering a comprehensive understanding of the world's diverse cultures and religions. Embracing Islam as a strand of substantive knowledge not only promotes religious literacy but also forms a bridge between Abrahamic faiths. By exploring the commonalities and differences among these religions, young learners develop an early appreciation for linking knowledge between the religions. This will be even more so as they move into Key Stage 2.

Islam is a monotheistic religion founded on the teachings of Prophet Muhammad. Its core tenets, known as the Five Pillars, include faith in one God, prayer, charity, fasting during Ramadan and pilgrimage to Mecca. Islam emphasises compassion, justice and submission to the will of Allah.

These will be better understood by your pupils through the use of images, videos, real-life interactions and experiences.

Quick vocab check

Islam and Muslim: a monotheistic religion founded on the teachings of Prophet Muhammad (PBUH). A Muslim is a follower of Islam, adhering to its beliefs and practices, such as prayer and charity.

Allah: the Arabic word for God in Islam. Muslims believe in the oneness of Allah, emphasising His attributes of compassion, mercy and omnipotence. This is an important term to emphasise: it is a direct transliteration from Arabic to English, rather than the name of a god.

Prophet Muhammad (PBUH): Islam's final messenger, receiving revelations from Allah. The spelling of his name in English can vary – for example, Muhammad, Mohammed – reflecting transliteration differences from Arabic. 'PBUH' stands for 'peace be upon him', a respectful phrase used by Muslims after mentioning prophets, especially Prophet Muhammad.

Quran: the holy book of Islam, believed by Muslims to be the word of God as revealed to Prophet Muhammad (PBUH). It contains guidance on moral, spiritual and practical aspects of life, serving as a fundamental source of wisdom and instruction for Muslims.

Eid: a festive celebration in Islam marking the end of Ramadan. It includes special prayers, feasts and giving to charity. Eid al-Fitr and Eid al-Adha are significant Eid celebrations in Islam.

Ramadan: the Islamic holy month of fasting, prayer and reflection. During Ramadan, Muslims fast from dawn to sunset, refraining from food and drink. It's a time for spiritual growth, charity and community, ending with the celebration of Eid al-Fitr, a joyful festival marking the month's completion.

The Kaaba: located in Mecca, a sacred black cuboid structure representing the focal point of Islamic prayer and unity.

Minaret: a tower in mosques, which signifies the call to prayer and the connection between heaven and earth.

Rules and practices

Muslims follow a set of rules and practices rooted in the teachings of Islam which guide their daily lives.

The Five Pillars of Islam are fundamental: shahada (declaration of faith), salah (or salat) (prayer five times a day), zakat (charitable giving), sawm (fasting during Ramadan) and hajj (pilgrimage to Mecca). It is important to note that these terms are all from the Arabic language.

The Arabic language is significant in Islam, and it is important for educators to understand that the terminology used when teaching Islam comes predominantly from Arabic. Arabic is the original language of the Quran, Islam's holy text.

Prayer involves facing the Kaaba, a sacred structure in Mecca. Dietary rules, like avoiding pork and alcohol, reflect religious observance (and are more suited for Key Stage 2 teaching). Muslims also strive for moral conduct, embodying values of honesty, kindness and integrity. These practices foster spiritual growth, community cohesion and a sense of connection to Allah, guiding Muslims in leading virtuous lives in accordance with Islamic principles.

Symbols

Several important symbols hold profound significance in Islam, each conveying important layers of spiritual meaning. The most recognisable is the crescent moon and star, often associated with the Islamic faith, symbolising the lunar calendar. This is not an official symbol, but one associated frequently with Islam through arts, culture and flags.

These symbols collectively reflect the diverse and profound facets of Islamic beliefs, serving as visual reminders of key principles and fostering a deeper connection to the faith for millions of Muslims around the world. Further symbols can be explored once children transition into Key Stage 2.

Key figures

Islam has key figures pivotal to its history and teachings. Prophet Muhammad (PBUH), the final messenger of Allah (God), shared God's words in the Quran. In Key Stage 1, this can be shared along with the learning of Jesus Christ, who is also a significant figure for Muslims as a prophet and is mentioned in the Quran.

An imam in Islam is a respected leader who guides the community in prayer and provides guidance. They lead prayers at the mosque and often play a central role in community affairs. Imams are knowledgeable about the Quran and Hadith (sayings of Prophet Muhammad, PBUH) and serve as a source of wisdom and support for Muslims.

In Figure 5.1, we can see that the enquiry questions and vocabulary focus create a solid foundation from Key Stage 1 to Key Stage 2. The 'belief' strand here is key in cementing the disciplinary strand in your planning, particularly in Key Stage 1, where children are slowly exploring their analytical skills, while obtaining the (substantive) knowledge and facts.

The assessment statements of 'I can show some understanding…' aid in developing foundational knowledge for children. An example may look as follows:

FIGURE 5.1: Key Stage 1 & 2 – Islam: Foundational Knowledge
I can show some understanding of...
...what Muslims believe about Allah and the Quran

Substantive knowledge	Disciplinary knowledge
Key belief: Allah is the one God	Significance of the belief in Allah as one God
The 99 names of Allah	Importance of the 99 names of Allah
Allah is the creator and sustainer	
Key belief: the Quran is the word of Allah	Knowing the importance of the Quran in Islam
The origin and significance of the Quran	Analysing how the Quran is treated with care and what that shows about its importance.

...what Muslims believe about the Prophet Muhammad (PBUH)

Substantive knowledge	Disciplinary knowledge
Key belief: Muhammad was chosen to be a prophet	Knowing the importance of the prophet Muhammad (PBUH) in Islam
Key events, e.g. The Night of Power; the journey from Makkah to Madinah	Reflecting on the story of Muhammad as an example to Muslims.

Islam

1. I can show some understanding of what Muslims believe about God.

Backwards planning, a form of planning that can help teachers with reaching their desired learning outcome for pupils, structures the learning journey so that children are not just reeling off facts but also understanding the links.

- Who is God to Muslims? Understanding the Arabic word Allah, what this means and what language it comes from.
- Understanding that Muslims pray to Allah, in the direction of Mecca and the Kaaba.
- Understanding that the Prophet Muhammad (PBUH) is Allah's last messenger (creating links to Jesus Christ in Christianity, for example).

Lesson 1: Who is God to Muslims?

Disciplinary: beliefs

You will need
- a balloon
- examples of calligraphy of the name Allah
- paper and colouring pens and pencils
- calligraphy examples of Islamic art
- examples of artwork by other pupils – for example: www.natre.org.uk/about-natre/projects/spirited-arts/spirited-arts-gallery/2021/?ThemeID=96

Getting started

Begin the lesson by asking the pupils, 'Who matters to you in life?'

Children may begin to explore important figures in their life, such as parents, siblings, friends and teachers. Explore why they are important. This line of enquiry will be developed further when God is introduced.

Start to discuss the fact that these people are important to us, even when we cannot see them. Ask the children, 'Who else may we consider important, even if we cannot see them?' Some children may recognise that God is a figure related to this idea.

Use the balloon to help aid discussion and expand the children's critical thinking, by discussing what is inside the balloon that cannot be seen (air). Explain that although we know that the air is inside the balloon, keeping it inflated and in the correct shape, we cannot see it.

Introduce the new vocabulary of Allah, explaining its meaning and the language from which it originates.

Class activities

1. Show the children examples of calligraphy of the name of Allah and explore how this is used as artwork in mosques, at home and as decoration. Explain that examples of Allah through art in mosques and in homes is a reminder to Muslims of Allah's presence.
2. Invite the children to create a poster about who is important to them, including information about where they see them and why they are significant in their lives.
3. Explain to the children that Muslims believe that God is everywhere. Ask the children to produce artwork showing where they think people can find God/Allah. Use the examples of artwork by other pupils as inspiration. Ensure that pupils understand that Muslims do not depict Allah as a figure or person, as they believe that Allah is so great that He cannot be drawn in image form.

Plenary material

Conclude the lesson by asking the question 'Who is important to you in your life?', and then reiterate why Allah is important to Muslims in their lives.

Can children remember the Arabic word for God and recognise the metaphor behind Allah being everywhere, even if we cannot see Him?

Recording of learning

Children can either record their learning in their RE books or present the posters on a display in school.

Lesson 2: Who is Allah to Muslims?

Note: The lesson name is slightly varied, now that pupils have been introduced to the vocabulary of Allah.

Disciplinary: beliefs, living

You will need
- images of the word Allah depicted in someone's home
- 'Charlie and Blue ask about Allah and creation': www.truetube.co.uk/resource/charlie-and-blue-ask-about-allah-and-creation
- paper and colouring pens and pencils.

Getting started

Revisit the Arabic name for God – Allah – and where children may see or hear this word (in artwork, in a book, in a mosque).

Show images of the word Allah in familiar places, such as someone's home, to show that this is a part of the everyday Muslim experience. Ask the children whether any of the artwork matches the examples from the previous lesson.

Use the video story 'Charlie and Blue ask about Allah and creation' as the stimulus for the lesson. The video focuses on the name of Allah, along with the 99 names of Allah in the Quran.

Class activities

1. Watch the video 'Charlie and Blue ask about Allah and creation'. Use this as a discussion stimulus during a circle time.
2. Invite the children to choose one of the names of Allah suggested in the video to explore further, focusing on what they think the names mean. Talk with the children about how the names are in the Arabic language – the language of the holy book, the Quran.
3. Explore how Muslims believe that humans are Allah's khalifahs on this earth – they are here to care for the earth and everything on it. Discuss with the children how they look after their surroundings at home or at school and why.
4. Ask the children to produce artwork based on either Al-Khaliq (the creator) or Al-Musawwir (the shaper). What images would match these titles for Allah?

Plenary material

Conclude the lesson by revisiting the question 'Who is Allah to Muslims?'.

Can children recognise the metaphor behind Allah being everywhere, even if we cannot see Him?

Recording of learning

Children can record their learning on a display in the classroom or school. Sticky notes of children's comments during discussions can be recorded and saved in a class RE floorbook.

Lesson 3: What does Allah teach us about looking after important things?

Disciplinary: beliefs, expressing

You will need
- 'Charlie and Blue ask about Allah and creation': www.truetube.co.uk/resource/charlie-and-blue-ask-about-allah-and-creation
- paper and colouring pens and pencils.

Getting started

Use the video of 'Charlie and Blue ask about Allah and creation' as the stimulus for the lesson. Children should be familiar with this story from the previous lesson. Revisiting the names of Al-Khaliq and Al-Musawwir before rewatching the video will aid with revision.

Explore the idea that we are all khalifahs. Ask the pupils, 'How are we khalifahs in our own school?' Encourage the children to think about roles such as cleaning up our classroom environment, acting as school councillors and so on. Why do we have these roles and what do they teach us?

In Islam, Muslims follow lots of the rules in the holy book, the Quran. The Quran teaches Muslims to care for the earth, for animals and for each other.

Class activities

1. Make a class list of all the roles and responsibilities that teachers and pupils have in school that show that we are khalifahs. Children may create personal lists based on their roles at home too.
2. Invite the children to create a poster to encourage others to look after a certain part of the school, such as the playground, and why this is important.
3. Write the question 'How are we khalifahs in school?' in the pupils' RE books or in the class floorbook, and ask the children to write down their ideas. Provide pupils with sentence stems, such as 'In school, we are khalifahs when we...', to encourage full-sentence answers.

Plenary material

Conclude the lesson by revisiting the question 'Who is a khalifah?'.

Ask the children 'How are we khalifahs in this world?' and encourage them to use the vocabulary of khalifah to explain and explore how they can care for everything around them.

Recording of learning

Use floorbooks for recording learning or capture snapshots of discussions during the lesson using sticky notes. RE books can be used by the pupils to write their own statements.

Part 2

Key Stage 2

6 The disciplinary skills

As previously mentioned in relation to Key Stage 1, the disciplinary knowledge acquired in RE in primary school education in England refers to the skills, methods and approaches that teachers use as the underlying threads when teaching. These will help with your assessments and will keep the learning journey consistent, following a learning pattern that builds on your pupils' previous knowledge.

The suggested skills for many agreed syllabi have titles such as believing, expressing, living/exploring, engaging, enquiring and so forth. The key is ensuring that the skills and language used in RE in your school align with your school's overall approach, creating consistency and clarity in teaching methods and expectations across the subject.

Navigating the world: Religious education in Key Stage 2

In crafting an RE curriculum, teachers play a pivotal role in weaving a cohesive and meaningful tapestry of learning for their pupils. Clarity is paramount, and educators should articulate not only the 'what' but also the 'why' behind the units and content sequence. This clarity extends from the foundational knowledge laid in Key Stage 1, forming the bedrock upon which subsequent learning is constructed. Revisiting a unit or lesson of work from Key Stage 1 as a form of pre-learning or revision is not something to shy away from. It can, in fact, be used as an opportunity to further your children's skills and knowledge before attempting possibly more complex ideas.

The decision to teach in units and to follow a thoughtfully ordered content sequence is important for both the curriculum content and organisation for the teacher. It is not merely a pedagogical choice but a strategic approach, aimed at scaffolding knowledge. Teachers should be able to elucidate the rationale behind the sequence, illustrating how each unit builds upon the preceding one. This coherent progression is crucial for pupils to see the development of their understanding as they cross from Key Stage 1 to Key Stage 2. For example, by exploring Islam in Key Stage 1, particularly through appropriate vocabulary and visual prompts, it is likely that when faced with more challenging ideas of, for example, prophethood and revelation in Islam in Key Stage 2, pupils will be able to build a link between the two. Examples of this are:

- Allah is the Arabic word for God (Key Stage 1) and it is Allah who Muslims revere as important and as being the founder of rules on this earth (Key Stage 2).
- Allah is the Arabic word for God (Key Stage 1) and the articles of faith include the mention of Allah as either a root word or suffix, such as subhanallah (all glory be to God) or Alhamdulillah (all thanks to God) in Key Stage 2.

The disciplinary skills

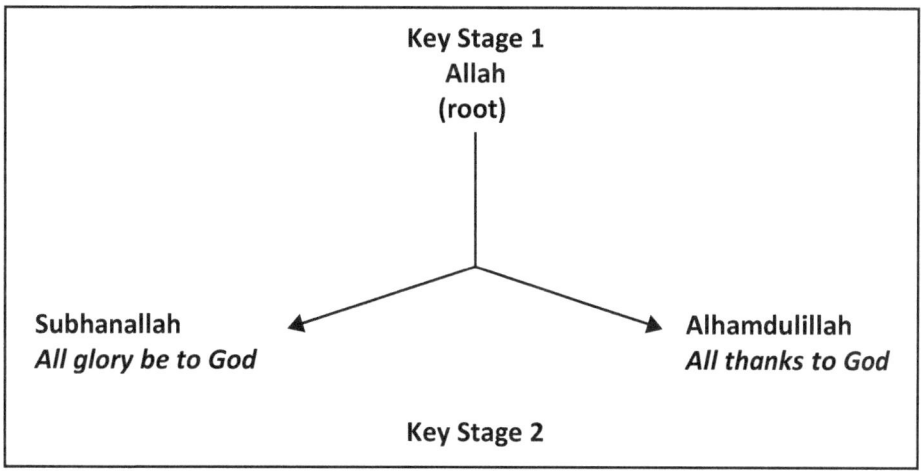

The threads woven in Key Stage 1 should seamlessly intertwine with those in Key Stage 2. This consistency is not only for the sake of curricular coherence but also for the benefit of the learners. As pupils transition into Year 3, they should discern the familiar threads, recognising when a lesson touches upon a belief or delves into the lived experiences of a particular religion or worldview. Creating those links is key.

What are the substantive skills in Key Stage 2?

When developing your curriculum, it is important to regard Key Stage 2 as a longer period of learning for your pupils; that is to say that you are given the opportunity to hone in on learning in Years 3 and 4, and then build on this even more in Years 5 and 6. Although one key stage, Key Stage 2 can be divided into two parts in order to organise the learning.

As previously discussed in the chapter regarding substantive skills in Key Stage 1 (see page 5), we are simply creating connections from one key stage to the next. The substantive knowledge in Key Stage 1 (that is, knowledge predominantly of the Abrahamic religions) is integral to further understanding and encouragement for philosophical questioning and reasoning as children enter lower Key Stage 2, in preparation for the upper Key Stage 2 challenges.

What do I need to know?

Substantive knowledge: The Abrahamic faiths in Key Stage 2

As previously discussed in relation to Key Stage 1, the expansion of knowledge for our pupils is based on building on previous ideas. We are able to do this by making sure that learning is revisited during lessons, and that pupils are given ample opportunity to review their previous learning and also to use this knowledge in discussion.

It is in Key Stage 2 that the opportunity to review pupils' learning from Key Stage 1 is welcome and, excitingly, teachers will have even more knowledge to work with. As pupils enter Year 3, their existing knowledge can be used as the foundation from which to teach going forwards.

Figure 6.1 provides examples of the knowledge that pupils will obtain in their learning with regard to the Abrahamic religions. It should be noted that this is not a substantive list for Key Stage 2; elements of this knowledge will be relevant for Key Stage 1 learning, and others will be used to build on in Key Stage 2.

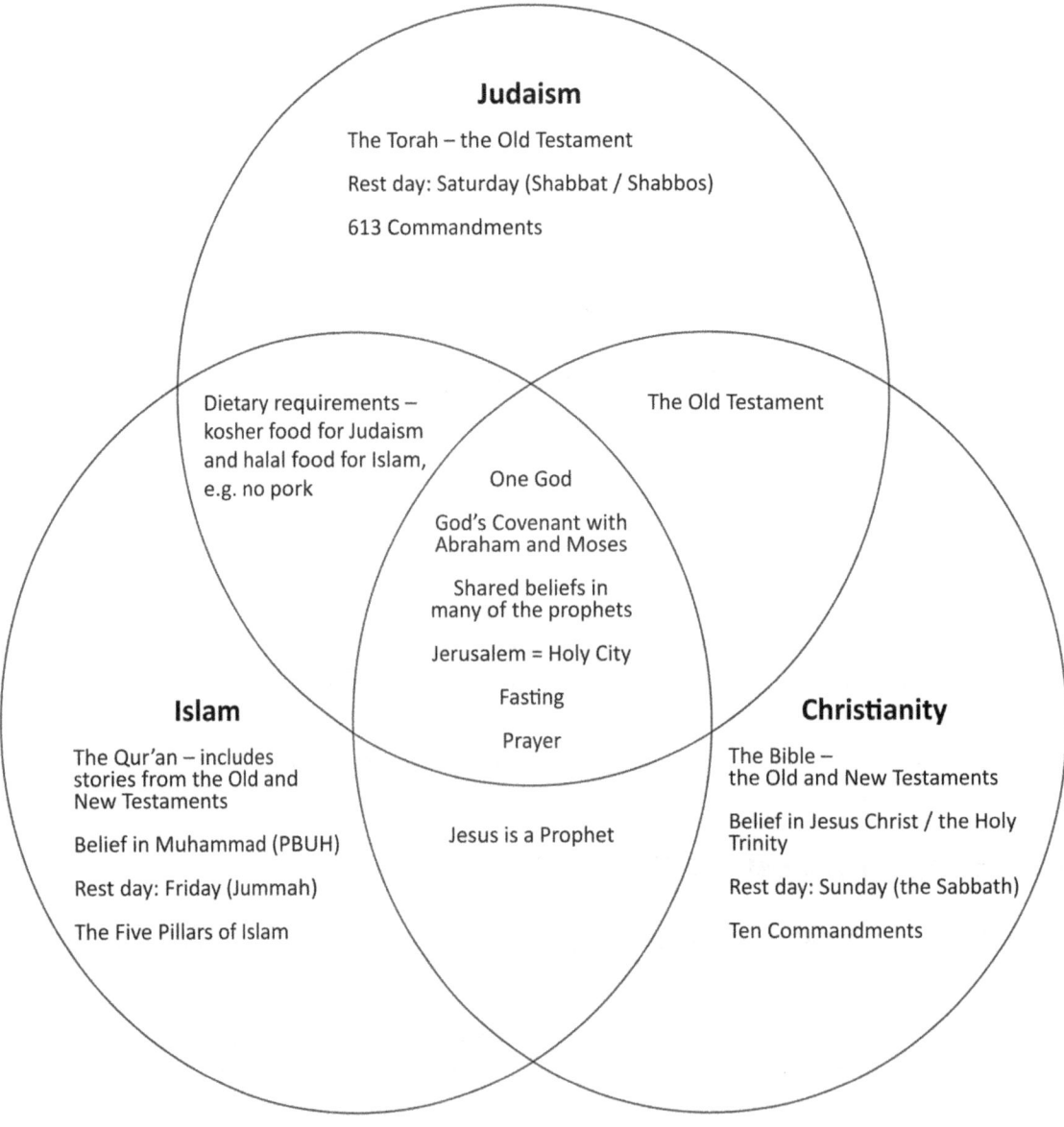

FIGURE 6.1: The links between the three Abrahamic faiths

The disciplinary skills

For example, knowing the Five Pillars of Islam is not foundational information in Key Stage 1; however, knowing that the Prophet Muhammad (PBUH) is the final prophet in accordance to Islam is. It is, again, important to understand that 'PBUH' stands for 'peace be upon him', a respectful phrase used by Muslims after mentioning prophets, especially Prophet Muhammad.

This is then built on in Key Stage 2, where the Five Pillars of Islam will make more sense, acknowledging that one of the Pillars – shahada (declaration of faith) – is acutely linked to knowing that the Prophet Muhammad (PBUH) is the final prophet.

> The shahada in Arabic text:
>
> أشهدُ أنْ لا إلهَ إلَّا أللهُ وأشهدُ أنَّ محمّداً رسولُ الله
>
> Pronounced: Ash-hadu alla ilaha illallah, wa ash-hadu anna *Muhammadar-Rasulullah*
>
> English: '*I bear witness that there is no deity (none truly to be worshipped) but Allah, and I bear witness that Muhammad is the messenger [prophet] of Allah*'.

7 Judaism

What do I need to know?

Following their learning in Key Stage 1, pupils will have been introduced to the fundamental tenets of Judaism. You now have a baseline from which to teach more about the Jewish faith, while integrating more questioning.

As always, it is good practice to refer to your local agreed syllabus to understand fully how Judaism fits into your school's learning context. It may be noted that various SACREs across the UK suggest that Judaism should be taught as a definite part of your curriculum, rather than as an option.

When pupils move into Key Stage 2, it is essential to revisit the vocabulary introduced and used in Key Stage 1. For example, understanding the difference between 'Judaism', 'Jewish' and 'Jew' is key for a deeper understanding of the Jewish faith in the upcoming learning.

Understanding the initial idea of the Torah being the holy book for followers of Judaism is important for pupils to then be able to develop a deeper understanding when they are introduced to other significant books in Judaism, such as the Talmud and the Tanakh, as Figure 7.1 shows. Further examples of this will be provided through lesson plans in this chapter.

Key Stage 1	Discover	The concept of one God
		The Torah
Lower Key Stage 2	Develop	The concept of one God, the impact of this belief, and the Covenant
		The Torah and the Talmud as sources of authority; the importance of reading the Torah out loud
		Key teachings of Judaism from important rabbis and the impact on Jewish beliefs and culture
Upper Key Stage 2	Secure	The concept of God being holy, just and merciful
		The Torah: translations and interpretations
		Different strands of Judaism: Orthodox, Conservative, Reform

FIGURE 7.1: Example progression of knowledge and understanding

Quick vocab check

Torah: the central and most sacred text in Judaism. It consists of the first five books of the Hebrew Bible, which are known as Genesis, Exodus, Leviticus, Numbers and Deuteronomy. Jews believe that the Torah contains the divine laws and teachings revealed to Moses by God.

Tanakh: the Hebrew Bible, consisting of three parts: Torah (Law), Nevi'im (Prophets) and Ketuvim (Writings). It is central to Jewish religious teachings and traditions.

Talmud: a collection of Jewish texts, consisting of the Mishnah (oral laws) and Gemara (commentary). It elaborates on the Torah and guides Jewish law, ethics and practice.

Moses (according to Judaism): a significant figure in Judaism, revered as a prophet, lawgiver and leader. According to Jewish tradition, Moses led the Israelites out of slavery in Egypt, received the Ten Commandments from God on Mount Sinai and guided the Israelites during their journey in the wilderness.

Abraham: considered the patriarch and founder of Judaism. He is revered for his unwavering faith in God and his role as the ancestor of the Jewish people. According to Jewish tradition, God made a covenant with Abraham, promising him descendants and the land of Canaan.

Mitzvah: a commandment or religious duty prescribed by God in the Torah. Mitzvot (plural) encompass a wide range of ethical, ritual and ceremonial obligations that guide Jewish life and practice.

Key facts and figures in Judaism and their significance

Abraham

Abraham is a beloved figure in Judaism, known for his unwavering faith and his special relationship with God. According to Jewish tradition, Abraham lived thousands of years ago in a land called Mesopotamia. He was a righteous man who listened to God's voice and followed His commandments.

God chose him for a special purpose. He promised Abraham that he would have many descendants and a land of his own. Abraham, along with his wife Sarah, left their home and journeyed to the land of Canaan as God instructed.

Despite their old age, God blessed them with a son named Isaac. Isaac was a miracle child and brought great joy to Abraham and Sarah. God tested Abraham's faith by asking him to sacrifice Isaac, but just as Abraham was about to do so, God stopped him and provided a ram for the sacrifice instead. This showed that Abraham trusted God completely.

Abraham's story teaches Jews about faith, obedience and trust in God's promises. Abraham is remembered as the father of the Jewish people and an example of righteousness and devotion. Through his story, Jews learn the importance of listening to God and following His guidance in their lives.

Moses

Moses, a baby born in Egypt, faced danger when Pharaoh ordered all Hebrew boys to be killed. His mother placed him in a basket and floated him down the river. Pharaoh's daughter found him and raised him as her own. As Moses grew, he learned of his Hebrew heritage and felt called to free his people from slavery.

God spoke to Moses through a burning bush, instructing him to lead the Hebrews out of Egypt. With God's help, Moses confronted Pharaoh, demanding freedom for his people. Pharaoh refused and Egypt suffered plagues until he relented.

Moses led the Hebrews through the parted waters of the Red Sea, escaping Egypt's grasp. They wandered the desert for 40 years, guided by God's pillar of cloud and fire. At Mount Sinai, Moses received the Ten Commandments, guiding the Hebrews' moral and spiritual life.

Despite his initial reluctance, Moses became a courageous leader, inspiring his people with faith and hope. His story teaches Jews about bravery, perseverance and the power of faith in God's guidance. Moses is revered as one of Judaism's greatest prophets and leaders, leading his people from slavery to freedom.

The Tanakh

The Tanakh, also known as the Hebrew Bible or the Old Testament, is a sacred text in Judaism. It is divided into three main sections: the Torah, the Nevi'im and the Ketuvim.

1. **Torah (Law):** The Torah is the most important part of the Tanakh and contains the first five books of the Bible: Genesis, Exodus, Leviticus, Numbers and Deuteronomy. It tells the story of the creation of the world, the history of the Jewish people and the laws given to them by God through Moses.
2. **Nevi'im (Prophets):** The Nevi'im consists of books that contain the writings of the prophets who spoke on behalf of God to the Jewish people. These books include historical accounts, poetry and messages of warning and encouragement.
3. **Ketuvim (Writings):** The Ketuvim contains a variety of writings, including Psalms, Proverbs, Job and the books of Ruth, Esther and Daniel. These writings cover topics such as wisdom, praise and the experiences of individuals in their relationship with God.

The Tanakh serves as a guide for Jewish beliefs, practices and values. It is studied, revered and interpreted by Jews around the world as they seek to understand their history, faith and relationship with God.

Mishnah

The Mishnah is an important text in Judaism that serves as a foundational source of Jewish law and tradition. Compiled in around 200 CE by Rabbi Judah the Prince, it consists of teachings and discussions on various aspects of Jewish life and practice.

Organized into six main sections called 'Orders', the Mishnah covers topics such as:

1. Zeraim (seeds): Deals with prayer, blessings, tithes and agricultural laws.
2. Moed (festival): Laws of the Sabbath and the festivals.
3. Nashim (women): Concerns marriage, divorce and some forms of oaths.
4. Nezikin (damages): Covers civil and criminal law and the court system.
5. Kodashim (holy things): Focuses on sacrificial law.
6. Taharos (purities): Addresses ritual purity, including mikva and family purity. A mikva is a ritual bath in Judaism used for spiritual purification. It is typically used for conversion, after menstruation or before significant religious events, to achieve ritual purity.

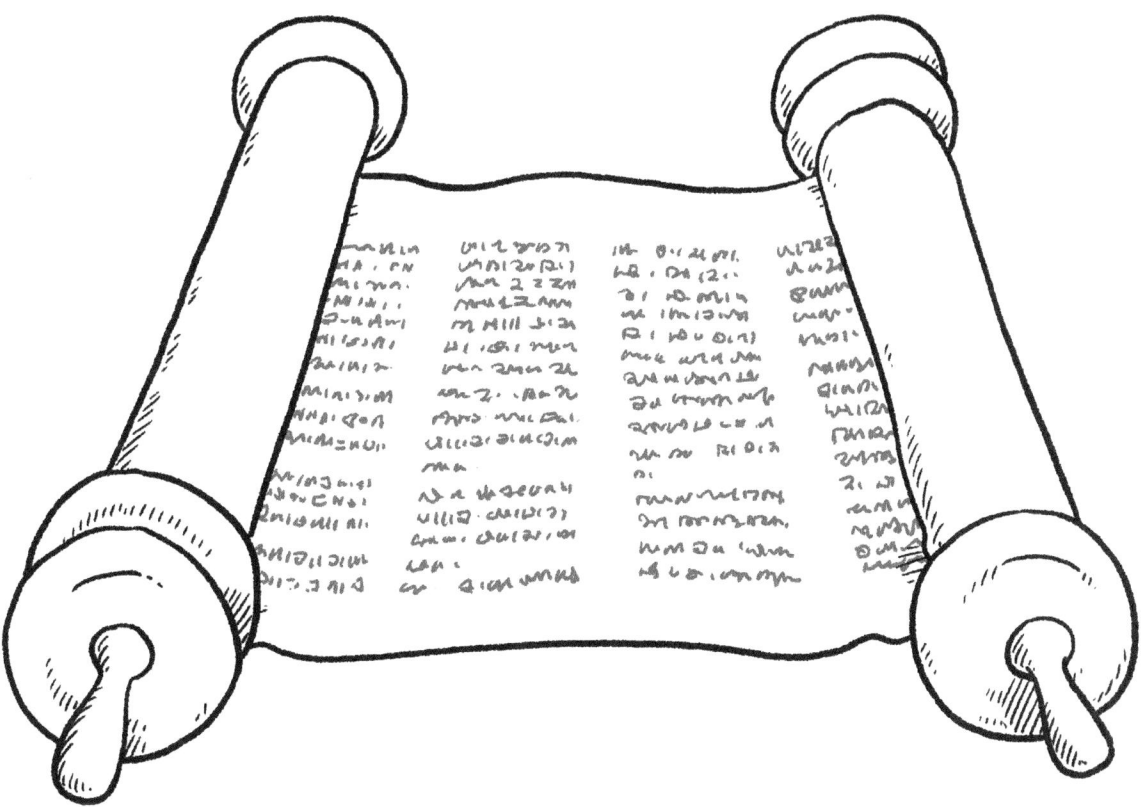

Lesson 1: What texts play an important role in faith for followers of Judaism?

Disciplinary: beliefs

You will need
- visuals of holy books, such as the Torah, Talmud and Tanakh
- a physical Torah or images of Torahs
- the story of Moses
- access to the following: www.bbc.co.uk/teach/class-clips-video/articles/zhs2t39

Getting started
Begin the lesson by discussing what important books the children know – these can be religious or non-religious. Guide the discussion into talking about the holy books of which they are aware. Compile a list on the whiteboard.

Keep the discussion simple and engaging by asking questions like 'What holy books do you know of?' and 'Why might a religion have a holy book?'.

Use visuals of holy books to engage learning further and to enable children to make the connection between the vocabulary and the object.

Class activities
1. **Torah scroll exploration:** Invite pupils to respectfully examine a Torah scroll up close. Explain its significance as the holiest book in Judaism. Discuss its handwritten text, parchment material and ceremonial handling. Encourage pupils to ask questions and observe the scroll's intricate details.
2. **Torah storytelling:** Share engaging stories from the Torah, such as the story of Moses. This could be a positive opportunity to incorporate role-play and allow children to act out the story to their peers. Encourage pupils to retell the stories in their own words and discuss each story's moral lesson.
3. Provide a space for pupils to discuss why holy books hold a significant place in religion, and particularly why the Torah is important in Judaism. This can be linked to their previous Key Stage 1 learning of the important symbols in Judaism.

Plenary material
Conclude the lesson by revisiting the initial question: 'Why is the Torah important to Jews?' This will be a question that you keep revisiting during the journey of learning.

Recap key points about Jewish beliefs and symbols, and why the Torah plays a significant role in Jewish practice.

Focusing on a story from the Torah, such as the story of Moses, provides an opportunity to explore the teachings of significant figures and their importance for followers of Judaism.

Recording of learning
Photos can be taken of the children object-handling and/or discussing images of the Torah, which can be stuck in their books or a class-shared RE floorbook.

Lesson 2: Why is the Torah so important to Jewish people?

Note: This is a great follow-up lesson from the Key Stage 1 Lesson 2: Jewish symbols and the importance in Jewish practice (see page 11).

Disciplinary: beliefs

You will need
- a physical Torah or images of Torahs
- images and/or physical copies of the Tanakh and Talmud
- examples of Hebrew script
- access to the following websites: www.bbc.co.uk/religion/religions/judaism/texts/talmud.shtml#:~:text=The%20Talmud%20is%20the%20source%20from%20which%20the,writing%20down.%20It%20includes%20their%20differences%20of%20view and https://youtu.be/dTiQb_3FGSE

Getting started
Discuss again the position of holy books in religion. What is their purpose?

Explain to the children that followers of Judaism have other texts that they consider important alongside the Torah, such as the Tanakh. Explain to the children that Hebrew is the language of the Jewish holy texts and show them examples of Hebrew script.

The Tanakh is a sacred text in Judaism and is often referred to as the Hebrew Bible. It is considered by Jews to be the written law. The word TaNaKh is an acronym made up of the three sections found within the book:

- Torah
- Nevi'im (or Nebi'im)
- Ketuvim.

It is not necessary for pupils to be versed in what each part of the acronym is, but it is good general knowledge.

Can children think why it is called the Hebrew Bible? This is an opportunity for cross-religion learning and linking.

Another cross-curricular opportunity is available here: are pupils able to link Christianity to Judaism on a historic timeline? This should provide a chance to link religions and their texts through a historical lens, particularly from Year 2 into Key Stage 2.

Class activities

1. Explore where Jewish laws come from in the Tanakh by watching the 'Where do Jewish laws come from?' video. Can the children name at least three laws discussed in the video and explain how these are relayed in daily Jewish life?
2. Look at the 39 Mishnah rules explored in the 'Where do Jewish laws come from?' video and discuss why they are forbidden and which rules pupils think would be more difficult than others to honour in modern life. A list can be created where there are two categories: adaptable to modern life and unadaptable to modern life. Explain why.
3. Divide the class into six groups. Give each group one of the six categories from the Mishnah to research and then present, as posters, orally to the class or as an IT presentation.

Plenary material

Conclude the lesson by revisiting what the Tanakh is, the rules in the Mishnah and how they are used in everyday Jewish life.

Children can swap research posters or find a partner from another group with whom to share knowledge about the Mishnah categories.

Recording of learning

Photos can be taken of the children presenting to the class. Posters of research can be stuck into the children's books or displayed in class.

Lesson 3: How were Jewish stories recorded?

Disciplinary: beliefs, living

You will need

- a copy of the story of Abraham for each pupil
- paper, pens and colouring pencils
- technology to film children retelling stories.

Judaism

Getting started

Discuss with the class different ways in which a story can be told. How many ways can they list? Think about examples such as books, oral traditions, through plays and podcasts.

Introduce the children to the story of Abraham. Explain that in Jewish tradition, orally reciting stories and rules was one way in which to ensure that stories were passed on from generation to generation.

Class activities

1. Read the story of Abraham as a class, and then provide the children with their own copies to read independently. What is the moral of the story? What kind of character was Abraham?

2. **Timeline of Abraham's life:** Ask the children to create a timeline of Abraham's life. They should include key events such as his call by God, his journey to Canaan, the birth of Isaac and the binding of Isaac. Encourage the children to illustrate each event and write brief descriptions explaining its significance. Display the timelines around the classroom and discuss the sequence of events and their impact on Jewish history and faith.

3. **Role-playing Abraham's journey:** Divide the children into small groups and assign each group a specific scene from the story of Abraham, such as his departure from Ur, his encounter with the three angels or his willingness to sacrifice Isaac. Encourage the groups to create short role-plays depicting their assigned scene. Allow children the opportunity to orally recite their section of the story to the class. Film the children's performances for them to watch back.

Plenary material

Conclude the lesson by revising the various ways of telling a story. Can any of the children orally recite a section of the story of Abraham that they were not assigned in the class? This will allow teachers to assess the children's listening skills.

Recording of learning

Photos can be taken of the children reciting to the class and stuck in their books. Filming the pupils while performing can also be used as a form of recorded assessment.

8 Christianity

What do I need to know?

The teaching and learning of Christianity in Key Stage 2 is an exciting opportunity to develop what has already been learned in Key Stage 1. It is important to remember that covering a subject is not the same as children thoroughly understanding the substantive knowledge that they have gained, and using this knowledge to access new learning and thinking.

Christianity is a significant component in almost all agreed syllabi, being used as both an example of religious tradition and an example of an organised worldview. During Key Stage 1, pupils will have learned about the traditions and practices shared by many Christians, and Key Stage 2 provides them with an opportunity to develop their understanding of the religion and to consider what it means to be a Christian and what this may look like in comparison to other religions.

As always, an essential foundation from moving between key stages is the revision of key vocabulary, which in turn will aid with the learning and use of new vocabulary.

Quick vocab check

Saviour: in relation to Christianity, a reference to Jesus Christ. Christians believe that he sacrificed himself in order to make salvation possible for human beings.

Disciples: in relation to Christianity, followers or students who learned from Jesus and who became his close friends.

Parable: a simple story that teaches a lesson, as told by Jesus.

Resurrection: in relation to Christianity, Jesus's coming back to life after death.

Crucifix: a cross, often with a figure of Jesus on it. It reminds Christians of Jesus's crucifixion, where he was nailed to a cross. It's a symbol of love and sacrifice for Christians, representing Jesus's death and resurrection.

Key stories in Christianity and their significance

In Christianity, a parable is a simple story used to convey a spiritual or moral lesson. These stories were often told by Jesus during his teachings, and recorded in the Gospels of the Bible. Parables typically involve relatable situations from everyday life, making complex spiritual concepts more accessible to listeners. This is especially poignant when teaching children, as using the stories as metaphors for everyday situations in their own lives allows for reflection as well as understanding key vocabulary in context. By using familiar imagery

Christianity

and scenarios, Jesus could effectively communicate profound truths about God's kingdom, morality, compassion and the nature of faith.

Parables often feature characters facing dilemmas or challenges, with their decisions or actions serving as lessons for listeners. For example, the Parable of the Good Samaritan teaches about compassion and kindness towards others, regardless of differences. Similarly, the Parable of the Prodigal Son illustrates themes of forgiveness and redemption.

Parables serve as powerful tools for teaching spiritual truths, allowing listeners to engage with timeless principles in ways that resonate with their daily experiences.

Lesson 1: What qualities make a good person?

Disciplinary: beliefs

You will need:
- a very large sheet of paper
- A4 pieces of paper
- blank playing cards or small pieces of paper to cut out jigsaw outlines – a set of jigsaw pieces per group (around four or five)

Teaching Primary RE

4. scissors
5. pencils and colouring pencils
6. the story of the Good Samaritan.

Getting started
Teaching the story of the Good Samaritan to children in lower Key Stage 2 can be both fun and impactful.

Draw an outline of a person on a large piece of paper. Discuss with the pupils the qualities that make a good person, and invite them to write their answers on the outside of the outline.

Discuss with the pupils whether they think that they share any of these qualities and what makes them a good person. Why? Can they share examples of why these traits are considered good?

Explain the meaning of the key vocabulary 'parable' and discuss with the children what these stories might mean to Christians. Do the children have books or stories that mean something to them?

Read the story of the Good Samaritan and ask the children why they think that the Samaritan is a good person.

Class activities
1. **Role-playing:** Divide the children into small groups and assign each child in the group a role to act out the story of the Good Samaritan. One child can be the traveller, another/others the robbers, one the priest and Levite, and the last child the Good Samaritan. Allow them some time to plan their role-plays, and then have each group perform in front of the class. After each performance, discuss with the children what they learned from the story and how they can apply its lessons to their lives.

2. **Compassion cards:** Provide each child with cards or small pieces of paper and art supplies. Ask them to draw or write about acts of kindness and compassion that they can do for others, inspired by the Good Samaritan story. Encourage them to be creative and think of ways in which to help people in their families, schools and communities. Once they've finished, collect the cards and display them on a bulletin board, titled 'Acts of kindness inspired by the Good Samaritan'. This activity reinforces the importance of showing compassion to others and empowers children to make a positive difference in the world around them.

3. **Story sequencing puzzle:** Create a set of puzzle pieces, each depicting a scene from the story of the Good Samaritan. These can be cut out and a set given to each group to use. On the pieces, either have key words based on the story, full sentences based on the story or images based on the story, depending on the ability and ages in your class. Divide the children into small groups and distribute the puzzle pieces among

them. Challenge the groups to work together to arrange the pieces in the correct sequence to tell the story. Ensure that the cards include key vocabulary such as 'Samaritan', 'God' and 'Jesus'. As they assemble the puzzle, encourage pupils to discuss the significance of each scene and how it connects to the overall message of the story. Once the puzzles are completed, invite each group to share their sequence with the class and explain their choices. This hands-on activity reinforces comprehension and sequencing skills, while engaging the children in active learning.

Plenary material

Conclude the lesson by revisiting the initial question: 'What qualities make a good person?' This will be a question that you keep revisiting during the journey of learning.

Recap key points about Christian beliefs through the story of the Good Samaritan. Revise the key vocabulary – salvation, parable, Samaritan and God – and ensure that pupils use these in the correct context.

Recording learning

Children can record their story-sequencing puzzles by sticking them either on large posters shared within their groups or in their own books.

Useful links

www.bbc.co.uk/teach/school-radio/audio-stories-the-good-samaritan/zf8w92p

www.bbc.co.uk/programmes/p011400q

Lesson 2: Why do Christians call the day on which Jesus died 'Good Friday'?

Disciplinary: beliefs, rituals

You will need

- pencils and paper
- art supplies
- excerpts from the Bible describing the events of Jesus's crucifixion.

Getting started

Begin the lesson by discussing with the pupils what can be inferred from the name 'Good Friday'. Why would a day be called 'good'?

Explain that Good Friday is called 'good' because it commemorates the day when Jesus Christ, according to Christian belief, willingly sacrificed himself on the cross (crucifix) for the salvation of humanity.

Despite the suffering and pain endured by Jesus during his crucifixion, Christians view it as a profound act of love and redemption. The word 'good', in this context, reflects the ultimate goodness and mercy of God, who offered humanity the gift of salvation through the death and resurrection of Jesus. Good Friday marks the culmination of Holy Week, a period of reflection and spiritual preparation leading up to Easter Sunday, which celebrates the resurrection of Jesus. Therefore, while the events of Good Friday are solemn and sorrowful, they are also seen as a demonstration of God's love and the promise of new life through Christ's sacrifice.

Class activities

1. **Symbolic artwork creation:** Ask the children to create symbolic artwork depicting the significance of Good Friday. This can be through a painting, drawing or using mixed materials. Encourage them to include symbols such as crosses (crucifixes), thorns, nails and hearts to represent Jesus's sacrifice and the meaning of 'good' in Good Friday. After completing their artwork, invite the children to explain their creations to the class and discuss how they see the goodness of Jesus's death.

2. **Scripture exploration:** Provide excerpts from the Bible describing the events of Jesus's crucifixion on Good Friday, such as passages from the Gospels of Matthew, Mark, Luke and John. Divide the children into small groups and assign each group a different passage to read and analyse. After reading, encourage them to discuss why they think that Christians call this day 'Good' Friday, despite the suffering that Jesus endured. Facilitate a whole-class discussion where groups share their insights and reflections.

Plenary material

Reflection journalling: Prompt the children to reflect on the question: Why do Christians call the day on which Jesus died 'Good Friday'? Encourage them to write down in their RE books their thoughts, feelings and questions about the significance of Good Friday in Christianity. After journalling, facilitate a group discussion, where children can share their reflections and engage in dialogue about the meaning of Jesus's sacrifice and the concept of 'goodness' in Good Friday.

Recording learning

Children's artwork can be displayed in the classroom or around the school.

Useful links:

www.bbc.co.uk/teach/school-radio/assemblies-ks1-ks2-forgiveness-prodigal-son/zn34239

Christianity

9 Islam

What do I need to know?

In Key Stage 2, pupils have the opportunity to build on what has already been taught and learned about Islam in Key Stage 1. This is an exciting time, where children are given the chance to develop their learning beyond the facts and rituals of Muslims, and to philosophise and ask questions such as 'What does it mean to be a Muslim in Britain?'. It is also an opportunity to learn about the shared practices of Muslims globally.

The approach in your lessons can look different depending on the skill (disciplinary) being explored. Islam can be explored through the skills of believing, living and thinking – all of which are highlighted in the agreed syllabi for many SACREs across the county. It is always worth revising your local agreed syllabus to match it with your school's curriculum.

Islam can be taught via stories and important figures, as well as the living example thread (see pages 59–60) to better amplify real-life encounters with living faiths, rather than a pragmatic focus on rituals only.

As always, an essential foundation for moving between key stages is the revision of key vocabulary, which in turn aids the learning and use of new vocabulary.

Quick vocab check

Pilgrimage: in Islam, a journey to the holy city of Mecca that Muslims make at least once in their lifetime. The pilgrimage is called the Hajj and involves rituals like circling the Kaaba and praying. It's a special time for Muslims to connect with Allah and their faith.

Kaaba: a sacred building located in Mecca, Saudi Arabia, and the holiest site in Islam. It is a cube-shaped building draped in black cloth, believed to have been built by Prophet Abraham. Muslims face the Kaaba during prayers and visit it during pilgrimage (hajj).

Makkah/Mecca: the holiest city in Islam, located in Saudi Arabia. It's where the Kaaba, the most sacred mosque, is located. Muslims face towards Makkah when they pray. It's the destination of the Hajj pilgrimage and holds great significance in Islamic history.

Ummah: the community of Muslims around the world. It can be thought of as a big family where everyone supports and cares for each other. Muslims feel a strong bond with fellow members of the ummah, united by their faith in Allah and the teachings of Islam.

Iman: faith or belief in Islam. It's about trusting in Allah and following His guidance. Having strong iman means having confidence in Allah's wisdom and mercy. Iman is an essential part of being Muslim and shapes how Muslims live their lives.

> **SAW/PBUH:** whenever Muslims say the Prophet Muhammad's name, they believe that it should be followed by a special phrase, abbreviated to SAW or PBUH in writing. The meaning of the Arabic phrase *sallallahu alayhi wa sallam* (abbreviation SAW) is 'may Allah honour him and grant him peace' or 'peace and blessings of Allah be upon him'.

Significant figures and pillars of Islam

The Prophet Muhammad

The Prophet Muhammad (PBUH), often referred to as the Prophet Mohammed (transliterated spellings vary), was a very important figure in the religion of Islam. Born in the city of Mecca in the year 570 CE, he grew up to become a wise and respected leader. He is considered the last prophet in Islam, chosen by Allah to deliver His final message to humanity.

As a young man, Muhammad spent much of his time in reflection and prayer, seeking answers to life's big questions. At the age of 40, while meditating in a cave on Mount Hira, he received his first revelation from Allah through the Angel Gabriel. This marked the beginning of his mission as a prophet.

Muhammad's message was one of monotheism, emphasising the worship of one God, Allah, and rejecting the worship of idols that was prevalent in Arabia at the time. He taught people to live lives of piety, honesty and compassion, and to care for the poor and vulnerable in society.

Despite facing opposition and persecution from some of the powerful tribes in Mecca, Muhammad continued to preach his message with patience and perseverance. Over time, more and more people began to accept Islam and join the growing community of believers, known as Muslims.

In 622 CE, due to increasing hostility from the people of Mecca, Muhammad and his followers migrated to the city of Medina. This event, known as the Hijrah, marks the beginning of the Islamic calendar. In Medina, Muhammad established a society based on justice, equality and cooperation among its diverse inhabitants.

Muhammad's leadership brought about significant social and moral reforms in Arabia, including the abolition of practices such as infanticide, slavery and exploitation of the poor. He also laid the foundations for a strong and united Muslim community, known as the ummah.

Throughout his life, Muhammad faced many challenges and hardships, but he remained steadfast in his commitment to spreading the message of Islam. He was known for his humility, kindness and concern for the welfare of others.

Prophet Muhammad passed away in the year 632 CE, leaving behind a legacy of faith, compassion and social justice. His teachings continue to inspire millions of people around the world to this day, and he is revered as a role model for Muslims of all ages.

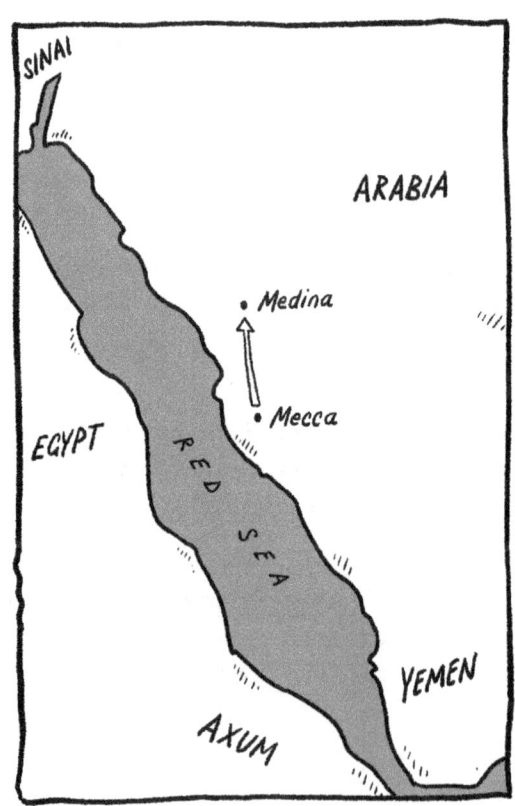

The Five Pillars of Islam

The Five Pillars of Islam are five important acts of worship Muslims follow. They are like the foundations of a building, holding up the structure of the Islamic faith. Let's explore each pillar and understand what it means:

Shahada (faith)
The Shahada is the declaration of faith that all Muslims recite and is as follows: 'There is no god but Allah, and Muhammad is His messenger.' This means that Muslims believe in one God, Allah, and that Muhammad is His prophet. It's like saying, 'I believe in Allah, and I believe that Muhammad told us about Him.' Muslims say the Shahada to show their commitment to their faith.

Living example: Every day, Muslims say the Shahada during their prayers. They might say it quietly to themselves or with others at the mosque. It reminds them of their belief in Allah and their connection to the teachings of Muhammad.

Salah (prayer)
Salah is the ritual prayer that Muslims perform five times a day. These prayers are called Fajr (dawn), Dhuhr (midday), Asr (afternoon), Maghrib (evening) and Isha (night). Muslims face towards the Kaaba in Mecca when they pray. Salah is a way for Muslims to communicate with Allah, express gratitude and seek guidance.

Living example: A Muslim might perform Salah in the morning before going to school, during their lunch break, after school, in the evening and before going to bed. They wash themselves, face towards Mecca and recite verses from the Quran, bowing and prostrating as part of their worship.

Zakat (charity)
Zakat is the act of giving to those in need. Muslims who have enough money are required to give a portion of it to help others. It's like sharing what you have with people who don't have enough. Zakat is a way to show compassion and support for those less fortunate.

Living example: During the month of Ramadan, Muslims calculate how much money they have and give a portion of it to charity. They might donate to organisations that help the poor, provide food for the hungry or support schools for children in need.

Sawm (fasting)
Sawm is the practice of fasting during the month of Ramadan, the ninth month of the Islamic lunar calendar. Muslims fast from dawn until sunset, abstaining from food, drink and other physical needs. Fasting teaches self-discipline, empathy for the less fortunate and gratitude for the blessings of Allah.

Living example: During Ramadan, Muslims wake up before dawn to eat a meal called Suhoor. Throughout the day, they refrain from eating or drinking until sunset, when they break their fast with a meal called Iftar. Fasting helps Muslims to focus on their spirituality and strengthen their connection with Allah.

Hajj (pilgrimage)

Hajj is the pilgrimage to the holy city of Mecca in Saudi Arabia that Muslims must perform at least once in their lifetime if they are physically and financially able. It takes place during the Islamic month of Dhu al-Hijjah. Hajj is a journey of spiritual significance, unity and devotion to Allah.

Living example: During Hajj, Muslims from all over the world gather in Mecca to perform rituals like circling the Kaaba, praying at Mount Arafat and symbolically stoning the devil. By completing the Hajj, Muslims feel a sense of closeness to Allah and unity with their fellow believers.

These Five Pillars of Islam are like the guiding principles that help Muslims to live their lives according to the teachings of Islam. They provide a framework for worship, ethical behaviour and spiritual growth, shaping the beliefs and practices of Muslims around the world.

Lesson 1: How do the pillars of Islam help Muslims to plan their lives?

Disciplinary: living

You will need

- paper and colouring pencils
- cardboard cut-out squares that can be turned into jigsaw pieces, five per child
- technology for recording role-play
- access to the following website: www.bbc.co.uk/teach/school-radio/assemblies-five-pillars-of-islam/zvvvp4j
- RE books.

Getting started

Watch the video of the Five Pillars of Islam with the class. Discuss with the pupils what the Five Pillars of Islam are and how they are applied to Muslims' daily lives.

Ask the children whether they can identify how some of the Pillars are linked to their previous knowledge of festivals – for example, sawm (fasting) and celebrating Ramadan and Eid from their Key Stage 1 learning.

Choose one or two Pillars as the focus for the lesson and use the questions outlined below as stimuli for discussion with the class:

Hajj:

- What is a pilgrimage?
- Where is Mecca located? (Cross-curricular link with geography)
- What are the rituals of a pilgrimage?

Sawm (fasting during Ramadan):

- Why do Muslims fast during Ramadan?
- How do you think that fasting helps Muslims to feel closer to God?
- What do you think that it would be like to fast all day?

Salat (daily prayer):

- How many times a day do Muslims pray?
- Why do Muslims face Mecca when they pray?
- How does prayer help Muslims in their daily lives?

Shahada (declaration of faith):

- What does the shahada say about God and Muhammad?
- Why do Muslims believe that the shahada is important?
- How do you think that saying the shahada helps Muslims to feel connected to their faith?

Zakat (charity):

- Why is it important for Muslims to give to charity?
- How does giving zakat help others in the community?
- What can we do to help people in need, like Muslims do with zakat?

Class activities

1. **Pillar puzzle:** Create a puzzle with five pieces, each representing one of the Pillars of Islam. On the back of each piece, write a brief description of the Pillar and its significance. Divide the children into small groups and provide them with the puzzle pieces. Encourage them to work together to assemble the puzzle and discuss how each pillar helps Muslims to plan their lives. Once completed, have each group present their findings to the class.

2. **Pillar poster:** Provide each child with a piece of paper and art supplies. Ask them to create a poster illustrating one of the Pillars of Islam and its importance in guiding Muslim life. They can use drawings, symbols and written explanations to convey their understanding. Display the posters around the classroom and facilitate a gallery walk, where children can admire each other's work and discuss what they've learned. This is also a form of assessment.
3. **Pillar play:** Divide the children into small groups and assign each group a Pillar of Islam on which to focus. Ask them to create a short role-play demonstrating how their assigned Pillar helps Muslims to plan their lives. They can act out scenarios related to prayer, fasting, charity, pilgrimage or declaration of faith (respectfully). After each performance, facilitate a discussion about the importance of each Pillar in guiding Muslim behaviour and decision-making.
4. **Pillar journal:** Encourage the children to reflect on how each of the five Pillars of Islam helps Muslims to plan their lives. Ask them to write or draw in their RE books to show their personal experiences, observations or insights related to each Pillar. They could also brainstorm ways in which they can incorporate the principles of Islam into their own lives. At the end of the lesson, invite volunteers to share their reflections with the class, fostering a sense of community and understanding. These reflections can be ongoing throughout multiple lessons.

Plenary materials

Conclude the lesson by revisiting the initial question: How do the Pillars of Islam help Muslims to plan their lives? This will be a question that you keep revisiting during the journey of learning.

Recap key points about Muslim beliefs through the chosen focus Pillar. This will help to build understanding of each Pillar through each lesson. If scenarios from the role-play have been recorded, it may be a good opportunity to rewatch a few as a class as a recap.

Recording of learning

If you are opting for presenting the learning through role-play, pupils' role-plays can be recorded using technology, allowing them to be viewed when needed. Posters can be displayed in the classroom and via school displays.

Islam

Lesson 2: How do Muslims feel as part of a community? What is the ummah?

Disciplinary: living, beliefs

You will need
- paper, scissors, glue and colouring pencils
- photos of various Muslim communities in the UK and globally
- newspapers and magazines
- A3 paper
- glue
- scissors
- clips of Muslims with various backgrounds, such as: www.bbc.co.uk/teach/class-clips-video/religious-studies-ks2-my-life-my-religion-islam/znmx47h
- printouts of the following flyer: www.natre.org.uk/uploads/Course%20and%20Event%20Flyers/Strictly%20RE%202018/Seminar%20B/ummah.pdf

Getting started

Begin the lesson by revisiting the Five Pillars of Islam. Can children remember the names for each of the Five Pillars? How might the Pillars be linked to being part of a community?

Introduce the children to the vocabulary of the ummah – what the ummah means in Islam and to Muslims, and what this can look like in everyday life.

Share with the children photos of Muslims in both the UK and globally, to show examples of how communities work together through their religion to help one another.

Help the children to understand the shared attributes to helping the ummah to stay connected, such as a shared language of Arabic* to understand the Quran, Islamic celebrations such as Eid and even the greetings, such as *As-salaam Alaykum*, which is used universally by Muslims.

It is important to note that not all Muslims speak Arabic, and this may be a topic of discussion with the class.

Class activities

1. **Ummah collage:** Provide the children with magazines, newspapers, coloured paper, glue and scissors. Ask them to cut out pictures and words that represent different aspects of the Muslim community, such as mosques, families, children and symbols of Islam. Invite the children to create a collage by arranging and gluing the images

and words onto a large piece of paper. As they work on their collages, discuss the concept of the ummah and its significance in Islam. Encourage the children to share their thoughts and reflections on how they can contribute to building a strong and inclusive ummah.

2. **Ummah circle discussion:** Gather the children in a circle and invite them to participate in a guided discussion about the ummah. Start by asking open-ended questions, such as 'What does the word "ummah" mean?' and 'Why is the ummah important in Islam?'. This is an opportunity to show children videos of Muslims from different backgrounds and their experiences. Encourage the children to share their thoughts and ideas. As the discussion progresses, discuss the scenarios from the videos that highlight the importance of unity, cooperation and support within the ummah. Facilitate a reflective dialogue where children can express their understanding of the ummah and brainstorm ways in which to strengthen it in their own lives and communities. The article from NATRE will be useful for the teacher to read to the class prior to and post discussion.

Plenary materials

Conclude the lesson by revisiting the definition of 'ummah' with the class. What links Muslims together to form the ummah and what does this look like within a community?

Recording of learning

Through discussions, children can write down their thoughts on sticky notes, and these be added to their RE books or be used to create a class display.

Collages can be displayed in the class, in pupils' books (if too large to fit, photos of their work can be stuck in their books) or around the school.

Lesson 3: What is the ummah according to Muslims?

Disciplinary: living, beliefs

Note: This lesson works well as a follow-on from Lesson 2. It brings to life the children's discussions and research through experience of someone who lives their life as a Muslim.

You will need
- paper and pens
- question grids
- an imam or member of the local Muslim community.

Getting started

Inviting in a member of the local Muslim community is a positive opportunity for children to meet someone who lives their life through the Five Pillars and who can share their lifestyle and thoughts.

An imam in Islam is like a leader who leads prayers at the mosque. They are knowledgeable about Islam and teach others about the Quran and how to worship. The imam helps Muslims to understand their religion and guides them in living a good life according to Islamic teachings.

Begin the lesson by revising the vocabulary of ummah – what the ummah means in Islam and to Muslims, and what this can look like in everyday life.

Pupils will be able to use their learning from the previous lesson to aid the discussion.

Class activities

1. Prior to the visit, work with the pupils to fill in a question generator. This can be done as a whole-class input or individually in each child's book. The question grid helps pupils to compartmentalise their thought processes and execute higher-level questioning.

2. During the visit, invite the children to ask their pre-generated questions. This visit can also be done virtually if in-person is not an option. Visiting a mosque with the class is a valuable learning experience, as it allows children to see Islamic practices and rituals in person. They can observe prayer areas, the minbar (pulpit) and other important features, deepening their understanding of Muslim worship. Children should also have the opportunity to ask questions, generated from their learning, such as why Muslims remove their shoes or how the call to prayer works. This interactive experience helps to bring classroom lessons to life, encourages curiosity and promotes respect for different faiths and cultures. It can be followed by reflective discussions back at school, to reinforce what pupils have learned.

Plenary materials

Conclude the lesson by revisiting the definition of ummah with the class. From their meeting with the visitor, what do pupils now understand about the idea of ummah?

Recording of learning

Question generators can be stuck in children's books as a reference.

Teaching Primary RE

Lesson 4: How do Muslims express community through food?

Disciplinary: living, beliefs

You will need
- Ramadan meals around the world video
- ingredients for stuffed dates:
  - dates
  - cream cheese
  - poppy seeds
  - desiccated coconut (optional)
  - honey (optional)
- teaspoons.

Safety warning: Always check for food allergies before the lesson.

Getting started
Revise from earlier lessons the word 'ummah', explaining that it means 'community' in Islam. Explain how Muslims around the world consider themselves part of a global family that supports and cares for each other.

Talk about how the ummah is connected through shared beliefs, values and practices, especially the importance of helping others and being generous.

This becomes even more evident through festivals such as Ramadan, where Muslims from all around the world will be celebrating the same thing at the same time, but from their own cultural worldview.

Watch the Ramadan meals around the world video with the pupils to generate discussion about food, culture and how people are different but share the same goal.

Explain that iftar (the meal to break the fast during Ramadan) is where Muslims invite family, friends and neighbours to share food together, and it is also seen as a form of zakat (charity), where food can be shared with the needy, demonstrating generosity as a core value. Can pupils see this happening in the video?

Class activities
1. Explain that Muslims break their fasts during Ramadan by eating dates.
2. Give each pupil some pitted dates. Show them how to gently open the dates if they are not already split, creating a pocket for the filling.

3. Invite your pupils to use teaspoons to add a small amount of cream cheese to their dates.
4. For added texture and flavour, invite them to sprinkle a few seeds over the cheese filling. Alternatively, they can roll the dates in coconut or drizzle them with honey.
5. Take time to eat the dates together and to enjoy time spent together as a class.

Plenary materials
Ask questions such as 'Why do you think that sharing food is important in Islam?' and 'How does sharing make us feel connected to others?'.

Conclude by explaining that food-sharing in Islam is not just about eating; it's a way in which to show kindness, build relationships and strengthen the ummah.

Recording of learning
Photos of pupils' food-share and cooking can be taken and stuck in RE books.

Question generator

The question generator allows children to expand their questioning skills. This is a tool that has been used across various humanities subjects and aids in thinking beyond the basic question format.

The generator can be tailored for either key stage, and additional columns can be added or taken away. Below is an example of a question generator for Key Stage 2.

	is/was	does/did/do	should	would	could	if
What	What do Muslims celebrate during Ramadan?					
When	When might you hear the call to prayer?					
Who	Who is Abraham to Muslims?					
Where	Where is the Kaaba located?					
Why		Why do Muslims pray in congregation?				
How			How should a Muslim help others in the community?			

Part 3
The Dharmic religions

10 Introducing the Dharmic faiths

The Indic or Dharmic religions all originate on the Indian subcontinent, meaning that there are multiple shared philosophies and practices that overlap between them, as well as having their own individual ideas.

In the primary curriculum, and as per the guidance of your local SACRE, there is the general consensus that the prominent Dharmic religions of study are Hindu Dharma and Sikhi. These are generally suggested to be introduced and form a part of the learning from the beginning of Key Stage 2. The remaining religions in the Dharmic family, Buddhism and Jainism, are often considered for a more thorough study in Key Stage 3. However, that is not to say that these cannot be discussed in Key Stage 2, particularly in the later stages of Key Stage 2 with Year 5 and 6 children. They provide a perfect opportunity to make links between faiths, ask meaningful questions and understand religion on a geographical level.

Introducing the Dharmic faiths should take place in Key Stage 2. During Key Stage 1, pupils will have been mainly exposed to the Abrahamic faiths. That is to say that they have become versed in the idea of monotheism – the belief that there is only one god – and in key figures, such as Jesus and Moses, as well as various religious celebrations. The questioning and critical thinking styles that have been developed through discussions will be beneficial to the pupils when they are formally introduced to the Dharmic faiths in Key Stage 2.

What do I need to know?

The Dharmic faiths are a group of religions that originated in the Indian subcontinent and share common cultural and philosophical roots. Studying the Dharmic faiths provides a perfect opportunity to use map skills, not only to locate them on a map but also to fully visualise the relationship between these religions. It allows for a more obvious worldviews approach as you delve into the Key Stage 2 learning. A worldview refers to the lens through which individuals or groups understand and interpret the world, shaping their beliefs, values and practices. It encompasses religious, spiritual and secular perspectives, helping people to make sense of different people and their experiences, even if they have a shared religion.

For example, Dharmic traditions offer a worldview of the forest – Rama and Sita in the Ramyanan in exile and Buddha under a bodhi tree, for example. This study also provides an opportunity to compare and contrast the Dharmic traditions with those of the Abrahamic faiths, where the worldview of these is of the desert – Muhammad at the cave and Jesus in the wilderness, for example.

The term 'Dharmic' is derived from the Sanskrit word **dharma**, which encompasses the principles of duty, righteousness, compassion and moral law that govern the universe according to these faiths.

Introducing the Dharmic faiths

The major Dharmic faiths include Hinduism, Buddhism, Jainism and Sikhism. It is important to note that the suffix -ism is contested by teachers and those of the religions as an English language suffix that makes the religion seem informal or derogatory in definition. Preferred terms will be explored further in this chapter.

1. **Hinduism/Sanatana Dharma:** Hinduism is one of the oldest religions in the world, with a rich background of beliefs, practices and traditions. Its name, Hindu, comes from the Persians, who named it based on the geography of the Indus River. Followers believe that their religion has no identifiable beginning or end and, as such, often refer to it as 'Sanatana Dharma' (the 'eternal way'). Hinduism encompasses a diverse range of philosophical and theological perspectives, including the concepts of karma (the law of cause and effect), reincarnation (the cycle of birth and rebirth) and dharma (moral duty and righteousness). Hinduism is characterised by its reverence for a multitude of deities, rituals, compassion for growth and sacred texts, such as the Vedas, Upanishads and Bhagavad Gita.

2. **Buddhism:** Founded by Siddhartha Gautama, known as the Buddha, Buddhism emerged as a distinct religious tradition in the fifth century BCE. It emphasises the Four Noble Truths – the truth of suffering, the cause of suffering, the cessation of suffering and the path to the cessation of suffering – as well as the practice of meditation and mindfulness. Buddhism teaches the importance of compassion, non-violence and the cultivation of wisdom to attain enlightenment and liberation from the cycle of birth and death (samsara).

3. **Jainism:** Jainism traces its roots to ancient spiritual teachings in India and is characterised by its emphasis on non-violence (ahimsa), truthfulness and asceticism. Jains strive to live a life of moral purity and spiritual discipline, seeking to attain liberation (moksha) from the cycle of rebirth through rigorous self-discipline, meditation and adherence to the principles of non-violence towards all living beings.

4. **Sikhism/Sikhi:** Founded by Guru Nanak in the fifteenth century, Sikhism is a monotheistic religion that emphasises devotion to one God (Ik Onkar) and the pursuit of spiritual union with the divine. Sikhs follow the teachings of the ten Sikh Gurus, as well as the Guru Granth Sahib, their sacred scripture. Sikhism promotes equality, service to others and the importance of living a life of honest labour and integrity.

Overall, the Dharmic faiths share common themes of ethical living, spiritual growth and the pursuit of liberation from the cycle of birth and death, each offering unique perspectives and practices for individuals seeking spiritual fulfilment and enlightenment. These are all ideas that can be discussed through your teaching as shared threads and commonalities.

As always, it is important to refer to your local agreed syllabus and where this suggests the introduction of the Dharmic faiths, which faiths and how. This chapter has provided a brief summary of each religion; it is likely that your lessons will focus on only one or two of the religions, in accordance with your school's context and curriculum planning.

What should I know?

The substantive knowledge needed to teach the Dharmic religions is key in laying out the foundation for pupils' learning, in order for them to draw links between the religions and, more importantly, find the links themselves.

There are many shared ideas and philosophies between the Dharmic faiths, although they are often applied to different figures or stories. Through the study of the Dharmic religions, pupils will be introduced to new ideas and characters that will, hopefully, excite and engage them in their learning.

As always, it is important to refer to your agreed syllabus, which will reflect the demographics in your school and local area. For example, if your school is within an area that has a dominant Sikhi community, this should be evident in your curriculum.

11 Hinduism – Sanatana Dharma

What do I need to know?

When teaching Hinduism in Key Stage 2, teachers should understand that it is one of the world's oldest religions, with diverse beliefs, practices and traditions. Many adherents would also argue that they consider Hinduism more a way of life as opposed to a religion. Key concepts include karma (the law of cause and effect), dharma (duty) and moksha (liberation from the cycle of rebirth). Teachers should explore major deities like Brahma, Vishnu and Shiva, and introduce festivals such as Diwali and Holi. It's important to highlight the variety of practices across Hindu communities, while encouraging respect for this diversity. Using stories, symbols and rituals will help to engage pupils and build a deeper understanding of Hindu culture and faith.

Quick vocab check

Dharma: the natural order of the universe, encompassed through duty, righteousness and moral law in Sanatana Dharma. It guides individuals to live ethically and fulfil their responsibilities in society according to divine order. Each living thing is living out its own path through dharma.

Karma: the law of cause and effect. Actions performed in this life influence future experiences and determine one's destiny in subsequent lives. Hindus believe that your karma is impacted by your actions in this life, meaning that you may come back into the next life as an animal if your behaviour was deemed negative.

Brahman: the supreme, universal spirit, the ultimate reality and the source of all existence.

Incarnation: the manifestation of a deity or divine being in a physical form on Earth. Examples include Vishnu incarnating as Rama or Krishna.

Avatar: divine incarnations of gods on Earth to restore dharma and righteousness.

Reincarnation: the belief that the soul undergoes a series of births and deaths, moving from one body to another in a cycle of rebirths until it achieves liberation (moksha).

Trimurti: the triad of Hindu deities, representing the three cosmic functions: Brahma (creation), Vishnu (preservation) and Shiva (transformation). They symbolise the cyclical nature of existence.

Vedas: ancient sacred texts of Hinduism, composed in the ancient language of Sanskrit. They contain hymns, rituals, philosophy and spiritual wisdom, serving as the foundation of Dharmic religious knowledge and practice.

Introducing learners to the idea of Brahman as being one supreme power who manifests into multiple characters (avatars), with varying roles and responsibilities, is one of the first steps to take when presenting Sanathanis' beliefs.

A visual way in which to present this to your learners can be seen in Figure 11.1.

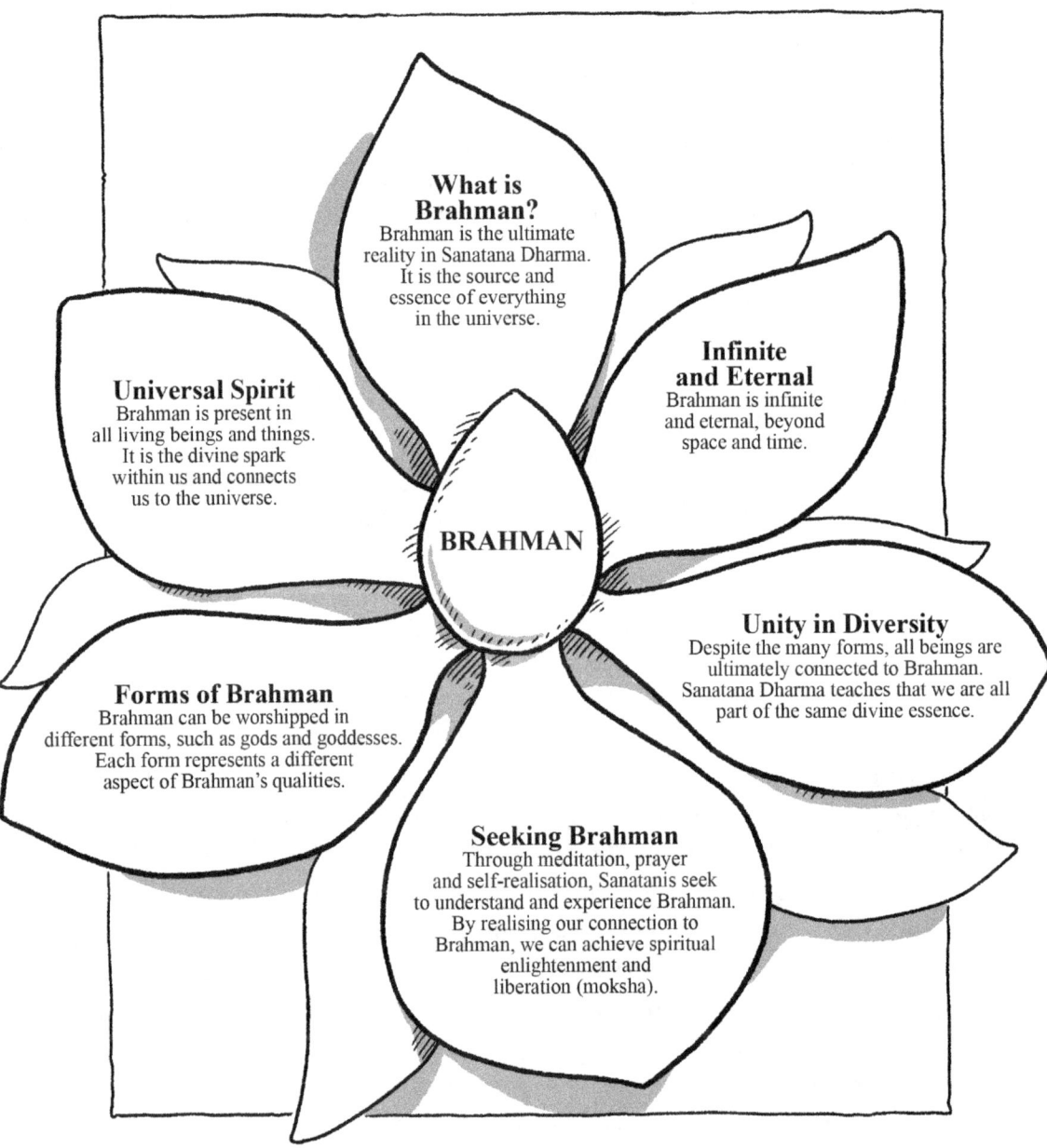

Dharma and its ideals are flexible and adaptable, being dependent on the framing of the ideas. For example, an interpretation of one idea or story may differ depending on the character focus.

The story of Rama and Sita

Long ago, in the ancient kingdom of Ayodhya, there lived a noble prince named Rama. He was known for his kindness, courage and devotion to righteousness. Rama was beloved by all, including his father, King Dasharatha.

One day, King Dasharatha decided to retire and crown Rama as the next king. However, Queen Kaikeyi, influenced by her maid Manthara, demanded that her own son, Bharata, be made king instead. To fulfil her wishes, King Dasharatha reluctantly banished Rama to the forest for 14 years.

Rama accepted his exile with humility, accompanied by his devoted wife, Sita, and his loyal brother, Lakshmana. In the forest, they encountered many challenges but faced them with unwavering courage and faith.

Meanwhile, the demon king Ravana, captivated by Sita's beauty, devised a cunning plan to abduct her. Disguised as a golden deer, Ravana lured Rama and Lakshmana away from their hermitage, leaving Sita vulnerable. Seizing the opportunity, Ravana kidnapped Sita and whisked her away to his kingdom of Lanka.

Heartbroken and determined to rescue his beloved wife, Rama sought the help of the monkey king Hanuman and his army of monkeys. With their assistance, Rama crossed the vast ocean to reach Lanka and waged a fierce battle against Ravana and his demon forces.

After a gruelling fight, Rama emerged victorious, slaying Ravana and rescuing Sita. Overjoyed, Rama and Sita reunited, their love stronger than ever. With Hanuman's help, they returned to Ayodhya, where Rama was joyously welcomed as the rightful king.

The people of Ayodhya celebrated Rama's coronation joyfully, rejoicing in the triumph of good over evil. Rama ruled with wisdom and justice, bringing prosperity and harmony to his kingdom.

The importance behind children reading and hearing the story of Rama and Sita is found through the characters of Rama (the hero) and Sita (the heroine), who embody ideals of virtue, fidelity and loyalty. Their story is often seen as an allegory of the struggle between good and evil, and it is a source of inspiration for countless generations. The story plays a crucial role in Hindu theology and philosophy, providing insights into dharma (duty/righteousness), ethics and moral values. Rama's commitment to his dharma – his duty as a son, husband and king – illustrates the importance of following one's responsibilities even in the face of adversity. Sita's unwavering devotion and strength reflect the ideal of loyalty and virtue, for example.

Lesson 1: What does life after death look like for Sanatana Dharma believers?

Disciplinary: belief

You will need
- paper and colouring pencils
- technology for recording role-plays
- scenario cards (see below)
- access to the following: www.bbc.co.uk/teach/class-clips-video/articles/zn68qp3

Getting started

Begin the lesson by discussing with the pupils who the followers of Sanatana Dharma (Hindus) are, and use a map to show where the religion came from geographically. The term 'Sanatana Dharma' is often used interchangeably with 'Hinduism', but it carries distinct connotations and historical significance that some prefer over the latter term. 'Sanatana' translates to 'eternal' and 'Dharma' refers to duty, law or moral order. Together, 'Sanatana Dharma' conveys the idea of an eternal, universal principle that governs moral and ethical behaviour.

The term 'Hinduism' was popularised during British colonial rule, and often carries implications of an organised religion akin to Christianity or Islam. Many practitioners feel that Sanatana Dharma more accurately represents the spiritual and philosophical essence of their beliefs, free from colonial interpretations.

Introduce the greeting 'Namaste' and explain to the pupils its meaning (I respect you). Explain that the Sanatana Dharma belief is that the same God is inside every heart and must be treated as one world-family.

Explain to the children that Hindus believe that when a person dies, their atman (soul) is reborn into a new body. This cycle of birth, death and rebirth is called samsara. How a person lives their life, doing good or bad actions (karma), affects their next life. The goal is to live a good life and eventually break free from this cycle to reach moksha, a state of ultimate peace and happiness.

Class activities

1. **Karma and rebirth art project:** Explain the concept of reincarnation and karma again, ensuring that the pupils understand how actions in one life affect the next. Ask the children to draw a series of pictures that show a person going through different lives. Encourage them to depict how good or bad actions influence each rebirth; for example, a kind act leads to a better next life, while a mean act leads to challenges in the next life. Invite the children to share their drawings with the class and explain the cycle that they have created.

Hinduism – Sanatana Dharma

2. **Reincarnation role-play:** Divide the pupils into small groups. Give each group a scenario card describing a life situation (see below for some example scenarios). Ask the groups to act out their scenarios and then imagine what kind of life the character might be reborn into, based on their actions. Invite each group to present their role-play to the class and to then explain how the character's actions affected their rebirth.

3. **Storytelling and discussion:** Play the video on the cycle of birth, death and rebirth. When the pupils have finished watching the video, ask them questions to ensure understanding – for example, 'What happens to people after they die according to Hindus?' and 'How did their actions affect their next life?'. Discuss the key concepts of reincarnation and karma, emphasising how good and bad actions influence future lives. Invite the children to create their own story with their own characters that shows the cycle of birth and rebirth. They could produce a storyboard to record the story.

Plenary materials

Conclude the lesson by revisiting the initial question: What does life after death look like for believers of Sanatana Dharma?

Recap the key points of reincarnation, samsara and karma. How might samsara and karma look in everyday life?

Recording of learning

Role-plays can be recorded and viewed when needed. Artwork can be displayed in the classroom and via school displays.

Scenario cards

Helping a friend with homework	Sharing your lunch with a classmate	Lying to avoid getting in trouble	Cleaning up litter in the park
Bullying someone on the playground	Stealing a toy from a sibling	Being kind to a new pupil	Ignoring someone who needs help

Lesson 2: What did Krishna teach about karma?

Disciplinary: belief

You will need
- the story of Krishna (see page 78)
- technology to record and take photos of role-plays
- paper, colouring pencils and pens.

Getting started

Begin the lesson by revisiting the key ideas of samsara, reincarnation and karma. Can the children remember what these terms mean?

Read the story of Krishna and Indra to the class. Explain that Krishna is one of many Dharmic avatars to whom many followers are devoted.

In the story of Krishna and Indra from Hindu mythology, Indra, the king of the gods, becomes angry when the people of Vrindavan stop worshipping him and instead worship Krishna, a young cowherd. In retaliation, Indra sends a torrential rainstorm to punish them.

Krishna, realising the danger, lifts Govardhan Hill with his little finger to provide shelter for the villagers and their cattle. He teaches them that their devotion and righteous actions matter more than offering sacrifices to Indra out of fear. Are pupils able to understand what the morals of the story may be?

The story illustrates the concept of karma, where actions have consequences. Indra's ego-driven actions, rooted in jealousy and anger, result in negative karma for him and suffering for the villagers. In contrast, Krishna's selfless act of protection and teaching about devotion leads to positive karma and the preservation of dharma (righteousness). It underscores the importance of acting with wisdom, humility and compassion, as well as understanding the interplay of karma in shaping destinies.

Class activities

1. **Role-play – Krishna and Indra's storm:** Divide the class into groups. Assign roles of Krishna, villagers and Indra within each group. Once the pupils have read and/or listened to the story of Krishna and Indra's storm, encourage pupils to act out the story, portraying the characters' emotions and actions.

After the role-play, lead a discussion using the following questions as prompts:

- What were the consequences of Indra's actions?
- How did Krishna's actions demonstrate karma?
- What lessons can we learn from the story about karma and righteousness?

2. **Karma wheel:** Provide each pupil with a blank sheet of paper.

Ask them to draw a large circle in the centre of the paper, which represents the wheel of karma. Ask the pupils to divide the circle into sections and label them with actions that result in positive or negative karma, using the story of Krishna and Indra for inspiration. They might choose to include actions such as selflessness, arrogance, kindness and humility. When they have labelled the sections, invite the children to illustrate each action. After completing their drawings, invite pupils to share and explain their karma wheels with the class.

Hinduism – Sanatana Dharma

Plenary materials
Conclude the lesson by revisiting the initial question: What did Krishna teach about karma?

Recording of learning
Role-plays can be recorded using technology to allow viewing when needed. Artwork can be displayed in the classroom and via school displays.

The story of Krishna and Indra

There once was a young boy named Krishna, who lived in the ancient lands of India. Krishna was no ordinary boy; he was believed to be an incarnation of the Hindu god Vishnu. From a very young age, Krishna showed remarkable wisdom and courage.

One day, as Krishna played with his friends by the river, he noticed the villagers preparing for a special festival. Curious, Krishna asked his mother, Yashoda, about the festival. She explained that it was a celebration dedicated to the divine cowherd Indra, who was believed to bring rain to the land.

Krishna, however, had a different idea. He suggested that instead of worshiping Indra, the villagers should worship the mountain, Govardhan, which provided them with food, water and shelter. The villagers agreed to Krishna's suggestion and prepared offerings for the mountain.

When Indra saw that the villagers had stopped worshipping him, he became furious and sent a powerful storm to punish them. But Krishna, with his divine powers, lifted Govardhan Mountain with his little finger to protect the villagers and their homes from the raging storm. For seven days and seven nights, Krishna held the mountain aloft until Indra realised his mistake and stopped the storm.

Through this act of bravery and compassion, Krishna taught the villagers an important lesson: that true divinity lies not in external gods but within themselves and the natural world around them. He showed them that by living in harmony with nature and recognising the interconnectedness of all living beings, they could find the true source of happiness and fulfilment.

From that day on, the villagers worshipped Govardhan Mountain and lived in gratitude for the blessings of the earth. And Krishna, with his playful smile and wise words, continued to guide them on their spiritual journey, inspiring them to seek the divine within themselves and all of creation.

12 Sikhi – Sikh Dharma

What do I need to know?

Sikhi, also known as Sikh Dharma (meaning the righteous path of living), is a monotheistic religion that originated in the Indian subcontinent during the fifteenth century. It is based on the teachings of Guru Nanak and nine successive Sikh Gurus. Sikhi emphasises the importance of equality, compassion and service to others. At its core, Sikhi teaches the belief in one God (Ik Onkar) and the pursuit of spiritual growth through meditation, self-discipline and righteous living.

A Sikh is an individual who follows the teachings of Sikhi and adheres to its principles. Sikhs believe in the oneness of God and the equality of all human beings, regardless of their caste, creed or gender. They strive to live a life of honesty, integrity and humility, guided by the principles of seva (selfless service), simran (remembrance of God) and sangat (community).

Sikhs also uphold the values of justice, equality and tolerance, advocating for social justice and standing up against oppression and discrimination. Overall, a Sikh seeks to embody the ideals of Sikhi in their daily life, striving to cultivate a strong connection with God and contribute positively to society.

Quick vocab check

Sikhi: the religion followed by Sikhs. It teaches love, equality and service to others. Sikhs believe in one God (Ik Onkar) and follow the teachings of the Sikh Gurus.

Guru Nanak: the founder of Sikhi and the first of the ten Sikh Gurus. He was born in 1469AD in present-day Pakistan and taught about peace, unity and compassion.

The Five Ks: five articles of faith that Sikhs wear as symbols of their identity and devotion to their religion. They include kesh (uncut hair), kara (steel bracelet), kanga (wooden comb), kachera (cotton undergarment) and kirpan (ceremonial sword).

Gurdwara: a Sikh place of worship. It is where Sikhs gather to pray, sing hymns and listen to the teachings of the Guru Granth Sahib. Gurdwaras also serve free meals to all visitors as a symbol of equality and community. The kitchen within the gurdwara is called a langar.

Guru Granth Sahib: the holy scripture of Sikhi. It is a collection of hymns and writings by Sikh Gurus and other saints. Sikhs regard the Guru Granth Sahib as their eternal Guru and show it great respect in gurdwaras and in their homes.

Guru Nanak and his story

Guru Nanak was the founder of Sikhi and the first of the ten Sikh Gurus. He was born in 1469AD in the village of Talwandi (now known as Nankana Sahib) in present-day Pakistan. From a young age, Nanak showed a deep spiritual inclination and a compassionate nature.

As he grew older, Guru Nanak began to question the social inequalities and religious divisions prevalent in society. He embarked on a series of spiritual journeys, travelling far and wide to spread his message of love, equality and devotion to God. During his travels, Guru Nanak engaged in dialogues with people from diverse backgrounds, including Hindus, Muslims and Siddhas, emphasising the unity of all humanity.

Guru Nanak's teachings centred around the concept of Ik Onkar, or the belief in one God, who is formless, timeless and omnipresent. He emphasised the importance of meditation, selfless service and living a life of honesty and integrity. Guru Nanak rejected rituals and superstitions, advocating instead for a direct and personal relationship with the divine.

Guru Nanak's spiritual insights and compassionate teachings attracted a large following, and his disciples became known as Sikhs, meaning 'disciples' or 'students'. Before his passing, Guru Nanak appointed Bhai Lehna as his successor, who became Guru Angad, the second Sikh Guru.

Guru Nanak's legacy continues to inspire millions of people around the world, and his teachings are enshrined in the Guru Granth Sahib, the holy scripture of Sikhi. He is revered as a spiritual guide, social reformer and beacon of light for humanity.

The Five Ks

In Sikhi, the Five Ks, also known as the Panj Kakar or the Five Articles of Faith, are five distinctive symbols that Sikhs wear as outward signs of their commitment to their faith and their identity as Sikhs. These symbols serve as reminders of Sikh values and principles, and connect Sikhs to their religious heritage.

The Five Ks are as follows:

1. **Kesh (uncut hair):** Kesh refers to the uncut hair that Sikhs maintain as a symbol of respect for the natural form given by Waheguru (God). It represents the acceptance of God's will and the rejection of vanity and pride. Many Sikh men and women do not cut their hair and instead keep it covered with a turban or headscarf.
2. **Kara (steel bracelet):** The kara is a steel bracelet worn on the wrist as a symbol of eternity and the unbreakable bond between a Sikh and Waheguru. It reminds Sikhs of their duty to live a righteous and moral life. The kara is worn on the right wrist.
3. **Kanga (wooden comb):** The kanga is a small wooden comb that Sikhs carry in their hair as a symbol of cleanliness and self-discipline. It represents the importance of maintaining personal hygiene and grooming. The kanga is used to keep the hair clean and tidy, reflecting the Sikh value of purity and orderliness.
4. **Kachera (cotton undergarment):** The kachera is a pair of cotton undergarments worn by Sikh men and women as a symbol of modesty. It serves as a reminder to control one's desires and maintain moral integrity. The kachera also provides practical benefits, such as comfort and flexibility, especially during physical activities.
5. **Kirpan (ceremonial sword):** The kirpan is a ceremonial sword carried by baptised Sikhs as a symbol of courage, self-defence and readiness to protect the oppressed and uphold justice. It represents the Sikh commitment to stand up against tyranny and oppression. The kirpan is worn sheathed and is not intended for offensive purposes but rather as a last resort for self-defence and protection of others.

Together, the Five Ks form a visual representation of Sikh identity and values. They serve as constant reminders for Sikhs to live according to the principles of Sikhi, including honesty, humility, compassion and service to others. By wearing the Five Ks, Sikhs publicly declare their allegiance to their faith and their commitment to upholding Sikh ideals in their daily lives.

Lesson 1: What do the Five Ks mean for Sikhi in Britain today?

Disciplinary: experience

You will need
- magazines and newspapers
- scissors and glue
- paper and colouring pencils
- a Sikh guest speaker
- access to: www.bbc.co.uk/teach/class-clips-video/articles/znbhf4j
- a world map
- blank playing cards or small pieces of paper
- images of the Five Ks (www.sikhiwiki.org/index.php/Five_ks).

Getting started

Begin the lesson by discussing who the followers of Sikhi are: people commonly known as Sikhs, who adhere to the religion founded by Guru Nanak in the late fifteenth century in the Punjab region of South Asia. Use a map to show the part of the world in which the religion originated. A map of Britain can also be used to then show the link between Asia and Britain, by highlighting for the pupils areas in Britain that have significant Sikh populations.

Show images of each of the Five Ks to the pupils (kesh, kara, kanga, kachera, kirpan) and explain their meanings and why they are important symbols of faith for Sikhs. Play the video 'The Five Ks of Sikhism' to the class, so that they can see how these symbols are translated into British life.

When the pupils have watched the video, prompt discussion using the following questions:

1. How are the Five Ks linked to faith?
2. Which of the Five Ks can be used in daily life and which are only for specific moments in life?

Class activities

1. **Five Ks collage:** Provide the children with magazines, newspapers, coloured paper, glue and scissors. Ask them to cut out pictures and words or to draw pictures representing each of the Five Ks. Ask the children to label each collage/drawing and to explain the significance of each item.

2. **Guest speaker:** Invite a Sikh guest speaker to discuss the Five Ks and their significance to them personally. Pupils should prepare questions in advance in order to participate in a question-and-answer session to learn first-hand about the importance of these symbols in contemporary British Sikh life.
3. **Creative writing:** Ask pupils to write a short story or diary entry from the perspective of a Sikh child in Britain, describing how they incorporate the Five Ks into their everyday activities and special occasions. This activity will enhance empathy and understanding of cultural practices. Encourage the use of correct terminology and vocabulary for more accurate understanding.
4. **Matching game:** Create cards with images and descriptions of the Five Ks. Divide pupils into pairs and give each pair a set of ten small cards each: five depicting each of the 5 Ks and the others blank. Together, on the blank cards, ask pupils to write a description of each K. These can then be shuffled and pupils can match the image with the correct description.

Plenary materials

Conclude the lesson by revisiting the initial question: What do the 5Ks mean for Sikhi in Britain today?

Can pupils recall each of the Five Ks and explain their significance?

Recording of learning

Written work can be recorded in RE or writing books.

Lesson 2: The Five Ks focus

Disciplinary: experience, belief

You will need
- paper and colouring pencils
- laptops or tablets.

Getting started

Begin the lesson by revising with pupils the Five Ks learned about in Lesson 1. If necessary, replay the video 'The Five Ks of Sikhism' from the last lesson to remind pupils of their learning.

Class activities

1) Divide the children into pairs and ask each pair to choose one of the Five Ks to research. Ask each pair to research their chosen K.

- Ask pupils to focus on the following questions:
- What does this K look like physically? Does it have variations in style?
- How does this K look when worn in everyday life?
- Is this K for both men and women?

2) Invite the children to present their findings as a PowerPoint presentation, poster or piece of artwork.

Plenary materials
Children should revisit their work and ensure that it is saved in a safe place on the school network.

Invite each group to present one finding to the class, sharing their drawings, explanations and any additional facts. Encourage pupils to ask questions after each presentation to deepen their understanding.

Recording of learning
All work can be displayed in school and photos can be taken for inclusion in RE books.

Lesson 3: How do Sikhs follow the idea of seva and sangat in British society?

Disciplinary: experience, belief

You will need
- scenario cards (optional)
- paper and colouring pencils
- access to: www.bbc.co.uk/teach/class-clips-video/articles/z4qc8xs
- access to the virtual trip: www.360cities.net/image/golden-temple-amritsar

Getting started
Begin the lesson by explaining to the class the concepts of seva (selfless service) and sangat (community). Highlight their importance in Sikhism.

Play the video 'The gurdwara' to the class. When the children have finished watching the video, discuss with them how the British Sikh communities engage in activities like langar (community kitchen), charity drives and disaster relief efforts. Discuss how these actions reflect seva and sangat. Can they think of examples in their own lives that would fall under these categories?

Class activities

1. **Role-playing scenarios:** Invite pupils to role-play different scenarios where they can practise seva and sangat, such as helping a new pupil, volunteering at a community event or organising a charity fundraiser. This activity helps them to understand practical ways in which to implement these values in their daily lives. Scenario cards can be created and printed before the lesson or the pupils can choose their own scenarios during the lesson.
2. **Virtual tour:** Take the pupils on a virtual tour of a gurdwara (Sikh temple) to learn about seva activities like langar (free community kitchen).

Plenary materials

Conclude the lesson by revisiting the initial question 'How do Sikhs follow the idea of seva and sangat in British society?'

Are pupils able to define what sangat and seva are and how they are adopted in British society?

Recording of learning

Writing can be recorded in RE or writing books.

Lesson 4: How do Sikhs follow the idea of seva with food in the langar?

Disciplinary: experience, belief

You will need

- access to the following websites www.bbc.co.uk/newsround/49957253.amp and www.bbc.co.uk/teach/class-clips-video/articles/z4qc8xs
- ingredients and equipment to make roti:
  - 125 g wholemeal flour
  - 125 g plain flour
  - extra flour for dusting and rolling
  - 1 tsp oil
  - ½ tsp salt
  - 120 ml water

- a bowl
- a griddle or skillet
- tongs
- a heat source to warm the frying pan.

Getting started
Begin the lesson by watching with the class the clips about langar. Explain the concepts of seva (selfless service) and sangat (community) and discuss their importance in Sikhi.

Explain to the class that roti is often prepared and shared as part of langar, the community meal in Sikh gurdwaras, where everyone is welcomed to eat together regardless of background. Roti is a simple bread that is often made by volunteers and served to everyone as part of the meal.

Class activities
1. Combine the flour, oil and salt in a mixing bowl.
2. Gradually add the water to form a dough.
3. Give each pupil a small portion of the dough to roll into a ball.
4. Support the children to flatten and shape the dough to form circles with the thickness of a £1 coin.
5. Heat the griddle or skillet over a medium heat.
6. Place the dough in the frying pan and cook for one minute or until small air pockets start to form on the surface.
7. Use the tongs to turn over the roti and cook for another minute until the roti is slightly browned.

Explain that everyone is contributing their effort to make the food, just as people do in langar.

Plenary materials
Once the roti is ready, gather the pupils in a circle and encourage them to share the roti that they made. Discuss how it felt to make something together and share it with others, connecting this to the values of seva and langar. Prompt reflection with questions like 'Why do you think that it's important to help others?' and 'How does sharing food make us feel closer to each other?'.

Recording of learning
Photos can be taken of the cooking process and shared in RE books.

13 Buddhism and Jainism

Buddhism: What do I need to know?

Buddhism originated over 2,500 years ago, with Siddhartha Gautama (the Buddha) in ancient India, and is a major world religion centred on overcoming suffering and achieving enlightenment. The Buddha's teachings, known as the dharma, provide a path to spiritual awakening and liberation.

The core of Buddhist doctrine is encapsulated in the Four Noble Truths:

1. **The truth of suffering (dukkha)**: Recognises that life involves suffering, dissatisfaction and impermanence.
2. **The truth of the cause of suffering (samudaya)**: Identifies craving and attachment as the primary causes of suffering.
3. **The truth of the end of suffering (nirodha)**: Suggests that it is possible to end suffering by overcoming attachment.
4. **The truth of the path to the end of suffering (magga)**: Describes the Noble Eightfold Path, a guide to ethical and mental development.

The Noble Eightfold Path is divided into three categories: wisdom (right view, right intention), ethical conduct (right speech, right action, right livelihood) and mental discipline (right effort, right mindfulness, right concentration). This path leads to nirvana, the ultimate state of liberation and freedom from the cycle of birth, death and rebirth (samsara).

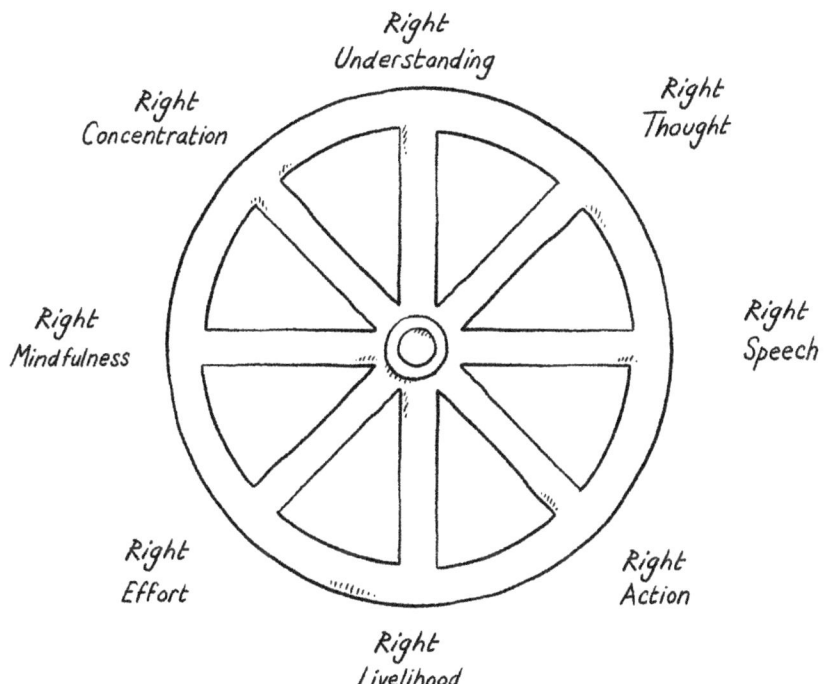

Karma, the law of moral causation, is central in Buddhism. It posits that intentional actions have consequences that shape future experiences, influencing the cycle of rebirth. Good actions lead to positive outcomes, while harmful actions result in negative consequences.

Buddhism emphasises meditation and mindfulness as crucial practices for cultivating insight and tranquillity. Meditation techniques, such as vipassana (insight) and samatha (calm), help practitioners to develop deeper awareness and control over the mind.

Quick vocab check

Buddha: the founder of Buddhism. His real name was Siddhartha Gautama and he is known as the 'Enlightened One'.

Enlightenment: a state of perfect wisdom and peace that Buddhists aim to achieve.

Four Noble Truths: the main ideas of Buddhism that explain why people suffer and how to stop suffering:

1. **Suffering**: the idea that everyone experiences pain and sadness.
2. **Cause of suffering**: the reason why we suffer is because we want things that we can't have.
3. **End of suffering**: we can stop suffering if we stop wanting too much.
4. **Path to end suffering**: the way to stop suffering by following the Buddha's teachings.

Noble Eightfold Path: the steps that Buddhists follow to live a good and peaceful life. These include being kind, telling the truth and meditating.

Meditation: a practice where people sit quietly and focus their minds to become calm and aware.

Karma: the belief that good actions bring good results and bad actions bring bad results.

Reincarnation: the idea that when someone dies, they are born again in a new life.

Jainism: What do I need to know?

Jainism is an ancient Indian religion that emphasises non-violence, truth and abstinence. It was founded by Mahavira in the sixth century BCE, although it traces its origins to earlier teachers called Tirthankaras. Mahavira, the 24th Tirthankara, reformed and revitalised the principles of Jainism.

At the core of Jainism are the Five Vows:

1. **Ahimsa (non-violence)**: The most important principle, it requires Jains to avoid harming any living being, including insects. This extends to thoughts, words and actions.
2. **Satya (truthfulness)**: Jains must always speak the truth.

3. **Asteya (non-stealing)**: They must not take anything that is not willingly given.
4. **Brahmacharya (celibacy or chastity)**: For monks and nuns, this means complete celibacy. For everyone else, it means fidelity within marriage.
5. **Aparigraha (non-possessiveness)**: Jains should minimise their material possessions and attachments.

Jainism teaches the existence of an eternal soul (jiva) that can attain liberation (moksha) through self-discipline and ethical living. The soul is bound by karma, the accumulated results of one's actions, which affect future rebirths. Liberation is achieved by purifying the soul from karmic particles through right faith, right knowledge and right conduct.

Jain practice involves strict vegetarianism, and many Jains also avoid root vegetables to prevent harm to plants. Monks and nuns follow even more rigorous practices, including fasting and self-denial.

In essence, Jainism is a path of renunciation and non-violence, aiming to free the soul from the cycle of birth and rebirth, leading to eternal bliss and liberation.

Quick vocab check

Jainism: an ancient religion that originated in India, focusing on non-violence, truth and spiritual purity. Followers of Jainism are called Jains.

Ahimsa: non-violence or not harming any living being. It is a central principle in Jainism, encouraging Jains to live peacefully and avoid causing harm to animals, plants and even insects.

Tirthankara: a spiritual teacher in Jainism who has achieved enlightenment and helps others to reach the same state. There have been 24 Tirthankaras, with Mahavira being the most well known.

Karma: the belief that a person's actions (good or bad) influence their future experiences. In Jainism, good deeds can lead to positive outcomes in this life or the next, while bad deeds can lead to suffering.

14 Creating links between faiths

Teaching the Dharmic faiths (Hinduism, Buddhism, Jainism and Sikhism) together at Key Stage 2 provides a valuable opportunity for pupils to explore the common themes and distinct practices within these religions. By drawing connections between these faiths, teachers can enhance pupils' substantive knowledge of shared concepts like karma, dharma (duty) and non-violence (ahimsa), deepening their understanding of how these ideas shape beliefs and practices across the faiths. Questions such as 'How are these religions similar?' and 'How are these religions different?' can be explored. This also provides an opportunity for a worldviews approach, whereby different perspectives with the same idea can be explored. Additionally, this comparative approach encourages disciplinary skills in religious studies, such as critical thinking, inquiry skills and making links to how people live. Children are invited to analyse similarities and differences, which helps them to build a nuanced understanding of the interconnectedness within world religions and appreciate diversity, while also developing skills in comparison, interpretation and respectful discussion.

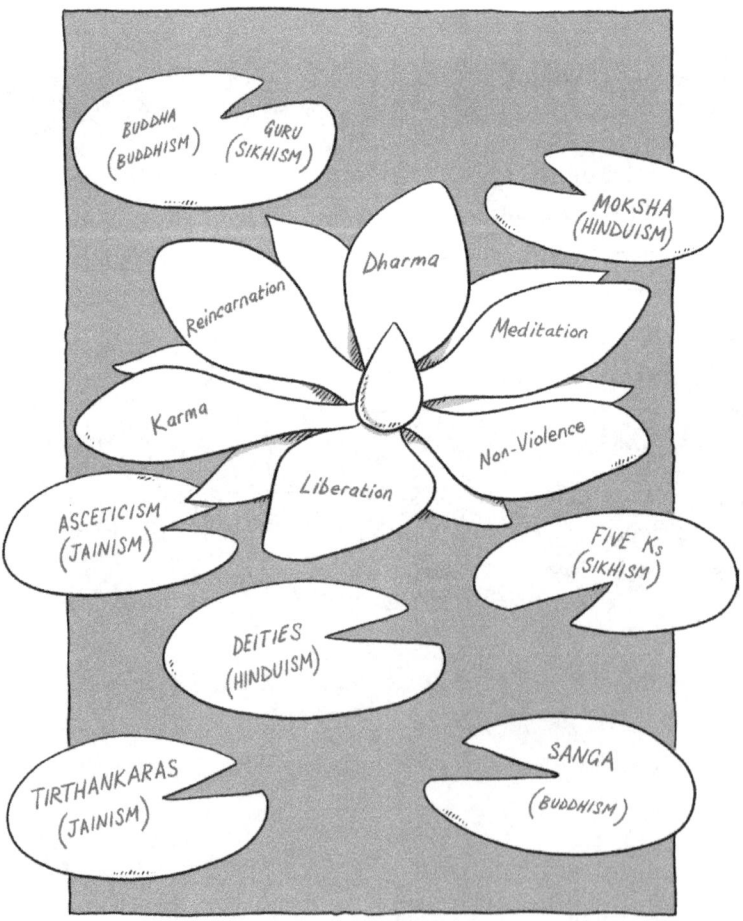

FIGURE 14.1: The lotus flower of Dharmic faiths shows the shared, central ideas joining into one flower, while the pads show their significant differences.

Lesson ideas for creating a link between the Dharmic religions can be found below. They provide examples of how connections can be created across learning, and how the threads of enquiry and learning can run from one lesson to the next without having to constantly introduce brand-new knowledge. It is important to utilise what the children already know in order to build and develop further enquiries, ideas and reflections.

Lesson idea: How is karma presented in Hinduism vs in Buddhism?

Disciplinary: experience, belief

You will need
- paper and colouring pencils
- access to the following presentation on karma: www.reonline.org.uk/resources/karma

Getting started

Begin the lesson by revisiting the concept of karma in Hinduism with the class, before introducing the idea of karma in Buddhism. If you haven't explored karma in Hinduism before, teach this lesson first (see page 77).

Explain that in Buddhism, karma means that our actions have consequences. This is a good opportunity to use the RE: Online resource, explaining what karma is through a Buddhist perspective. Good actions lead to positive outcomes, while bad actions lead to negative ones. Buddhists believe that karma affects our future lives and can help us to reach enlightenment by encouraging kindness, compassion and mindfulness in everything that we do.

Explain that in Hinduism, karma is tied to dharma (duty). Good karma, earned by fulfilling one's duties and ethical behaviour, leads to a better rebirth in the cycle of samsara (reincarnation). The ultimate goal is moksha: liberation from the cycle of rebirth. In Buddhism, karma focuses on intentions behind actions. Good intentions and actions lead to positive outcomes, aiding progress toward enlightenment (nirvana). Discuss as a class how these views of karma are similar or different.

Class activities

1. **Comparison chart:** Invite pupils to create Venn diagrams comparing and contrasting karma in Hinduism and Buddhism, noting similarities and differences. Use the RE: Online resource to aid with understanding karma from a Buddhist perspective.
2. Discuss how understanding karma can influence behaviour and decision-making. Encourage pupils to share their thoughts on how these concepts might impact their lives. Use the situation cards provided below to discuss how these may impact someone's karma. This is an opportunity for discussion as a class.

Creating links between faiths

Plenary materials
Conclude the lesson by discussing the similarities and differences in karma between Hinduism and Buddhism. Are pupils able to define what the differences are and give everyday examples from both perspectives?

Recording of learning
Venn diagrams can be recorded in children's dedicated RE books.

Situation cards

You are given too much change at the shop. What would you do?	You have not completed your homework, which is due in today. Do you admit this to your teacher?	You are keeping score at a game of football in PE. You lose count. What should you do?
You are playing with your sibling's toy and it breaks. Should you tell them or leave it?	You see another pupil being teased on the playground because of their appearance. What would you do?	Your friend asks you to let them look at your answers in a test. How would you react?

Lesson idea: Is the idea of ahimsa unique to Jains?

Disciplinary: experience, belief

You will need
- digital resources to record role-playing
- paper and colouring pencils
- the story of 'Love the animals': www.jainworld.com/education/jain-education-material/beginner-level/love-the-animals

Getting started
Begin the lesson by discussing the concept of non-violence and what this means to the pupils (this can be from a non-religious perspective). Examples might include choosing to be a vegetarian to reduce the number of animals being killed or being mindful of the words that they use when they are feeling upset or angry. Some Jains believe that even our words can be a form of violence.

Guide the discussion to talk about the idea that many religions have a concept of non-violence. Pupils may recognise some of the ideas from their previous learning. For example:

- **Sikhism:** Although Sikhs primarily believe in the concept of Sant Sipahi (saint-soldier), promoting defence of the oppressed, they also value compassion and non-violence. Sikhs advocate for peaceful coexistence and justice.
- **Christianity:** While Christianity doesn't explicitly use the term 'ahimsa', Jesus Christ's teachings emphasise love, forgiveness and turning the other cheek, reflecting a commitment to non-violence and compassion towards others.
- **Islam:** In Islam, the concept of compassion (rahmah) is fundamental. Although Islam allows for self-defence and the defence of others, it promotes peace, mercy and forgiveness as core values in interactions with others. The root of the word 'Islam' comes from *salaam*, meaning peace in Arabic.

After these initial discussions, introduce the concept of ahimsa. Ahimsa, meaning non-violence or compassion, is a principle found not only in Hinduism and Buddhism but also in several other religions. In particular, in Jainism, ahimsa is one of the core principals, central to Jain ethics. Jains believe in minimising harm to all living beings, practising non-violence in thought, speech and action.

Class activities

1. Read a Jain folktale or story illustrating the importance of ahimsa, such as 'Love the animals'. Discuss its moral lesson and how it relates to non-violence in Jainism. Can pupils make comparisons to any other stories from different religions?
2. **Comparison posters:** Divide pupils into groups to create posters comparing ahimsa in Jainism with other religions. They can use images and key pieces of vocabulary, such as karma and dharma, to highlight similarities and differences.
3. **Role-playing:** Invite pupils to perform short role-plays depicting scenarios where ahimsa is practised in Jainism, Christianity or other religions. After each role-play, discuss with the class how the principle of non-violence is upheld in each religion and its significance in promoting peace and compassion.

Plenary materials

Conclude the lesson by discussing what the idea of ahimsa is in Jainism, and how this can be interpreted in other religions and worldviews.

Are pupils able to identify any situations in their own life that link to ahimsa?

Recording of learning

Comparison posters can be recorded, either on large, shared pieces of paper or in children's dedicated RE books. Role-playing can be recorded for viewing as a class.

Part 4
Other approaches

15 Introducing Humanism

What do I need to know?

Humanism is a non-religious worldview that plays an important role in the teaching and learning of our pupils in RE lessons. Encouragingly, it has a presence in many local authority recommendations for Key Stage 2, which means that children are exposed to even more worldviews and opportunities to learn about ideas outside of religion too.

Humanism focuses on reason, science and human experience, rather than religious beliefs, as the primary sources of knowledge and morality. Humanism advocates for human rights, social justice and the importance of personal fulfilment and responsibility, without a deity.

Classified as a non-religious worldview, Humanism provides an alternative perspective to traditional religious beliefs, highlighting the importance of ethics and values derived from human experience and thought.

Approaching Humanism in RE involves presenting it alongside other worldviews to promote inclusivity and understanding. Teaching Humanism to your pupils will encourage critical thinking, through discussing Humanist responses to ethical dilemmas and comparing them with religious perspectives. Using discussions, debates and reflective writing will help pupils to explore how Humanists approach questions of meaning, purpose and morality.

Ensuring a balanced approach to how Humanism can look, depending on such things as a person's worldview, experiences and environment, helps pupils to appreciate the broad spectrum of beliefs and values, fostering a respectful and informed understanding of Humanism within the wider context of religious and non-religious worldviews.

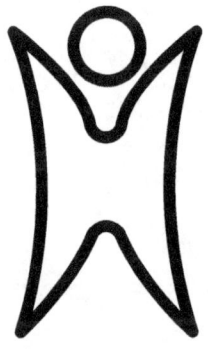

HUMANISM
Religion

Quick vocab check

Humanism: an approach emphasising reason, ethics and human welfare, focusing on secular and scientific approaches to understanding life.

Atheist: a person who does not believe in the existence of any gods or deities, often relying on science and reason for understanding the world.

Agnostic: a person who believes that the existence of gods or deities is unknown or unknowable, remaining open to the possibility but without firm belief or disbelief.

Reason: the use of logical thinking and evidence-based understanding to make decisions and solve problems, central to Humanist ideas.

Ethics: a system of moral principles guiding human conduct, emphasising human welfare, fairness and justice, without reliance on religious beliefs.

Secular: pertaining to attitudes, activities or other things that have no religious or spiritual basis, crucial in Humanist thought.

Empathy: the ability to understand and share the feelings of others, promoting compassionate and ethical interactions in Humanist values.

Autonomy: the principle of self-governance and making informed decisions independently, highlighting personal responsibility and freedom in Humanist ideology.

The Golden Rule

The Golden Rule in Humanism is a principle that emphasises treating others as you yourself would like to be treated.

It focuses on empathy, respect and reciprocity, encouraging individuals to consider the impact of their actions on others. This rule aligns with Humanist values of compassion and ethical behaviour, grounded in reason and human experience, rather than religious doctrine.

For example, in a classroom setting, a pupil practising the Golden Rule might see a classmate struggling with a difficult subject; remembering how they feel when they need help, the pupil offers assistance, perhaps explaining the topic or sharing their notes. This act of kindness nurtures a supportive and collaborative environment, reflecting the Humanist belief in mutual respect and the importance of helping others.

By promoting the Golden Rule, Humanism encourages a society where individuals consider the welfare and dignity of others, leading to more harmonious and compassionate communities. This principle helps pupils to develop empathy and ethical reasoning, essential for personal and social development.

Lesson idea: The Golden Rule – how can it be used in everyday life?

Disciplinary: experience, belief

You will need
- paper and colouring pencils
- access to the following site: https://understandinghumanism.org.uk/res_films/one-life-live-it-well
- examples of the Golden Rule from around the world, available at: https://understandinghumanism.org.uk/wp-content/uploads/2021/10/Golden-Rule-around-the-world.pdf

Getting started
Begin the lesson by explaining the difference between secular and non-secular views:

- **secular:** related to non-religious activities or beliefs
- **non-secular:** related to religious activities or beliefs.

Ask the children to make a list of secular and non-secular occasions – for example, birthdays, Christmas, marriage and so on. Discuss as a class.

Introduce the idea of Humanism and how Humanists believe that it is possible to live a fulfilling life without religion or the idea of a god.

Watch the 'One life, live it well' video. Discuss as a class what they think the main points in this video are. Then introduce the idea of the Golden Rule to the class. What do they understand from these rules? Can they find an example from religion to which they think some of the rules could compare? For example, the Humanist Golden Rule of 'Treat others as you would want to be treated' could be compared to the Christian biblical verse of 'Do unto others as you would have them do unto you' (Matthew 7: 12).

Choose one of the examples from the Golden Rules from around the world document for your lesson to focus on, and then discuss how this example shows the Humanist belief that you should treat others as you want to be treated, focusing on kindness and empathy in everyday actions.

This would be a good opportunity to compare a Golden Rule of your choice, first as a class and then using an example from a religion that the pupils have previously or recently studied.

Class activities
1. **Empathy role-play:** Divide the class into small groups and give each group a scenario where empathy and kindness can be applied, based on the Golden Rule.

For example:
- A new pupil joins your class, feels nervous and doesn't know anyone.
- A classmate drops their lunch accidentally and they don't have any more food.
- A pupil makes a mistake on a test and feels disappointed.

2. Invite each group to discuss their scenario, considering how they could apply the Golden Rule to support the person in the situation.

Plenary materials
Conclude the lesson by revisiting the Golden Rule in Humanism. How do the children carry out the golden rule in their own daily lives? Can they think of examples in and out of school?

Recording of learning
Photos taken of the class and group discussions from the empathy role-play can be stuck in pupils' RE books.

Useful websites:
https://understandinghumanism.org.uk

Lesson idea: How do Humanists celebrate happy moments in life and rites of passage?

Disciplinary: experience

You will need
- paper and colouring pencils
- Humanist naming ceremony story: https://humanists.uk/ceremonies/namings/blog/a-humanist-naming-ceremony-for-two-brothers

Getting started
Explain to the class that celebrating happy moments in life can also occur from non-religious perspectives. Can they name any examples?

Ask the pupils to name as many happy celebrations in life that they can think of – for example, graduating from university, passing your driving test, getting married and so on. Discuss with the class whether the examples are religious or secular and invite the children to contribute examples – either religious or secular – from their own lives.

Use some of the religious examples provided to compare how these are similar or different to those practised by Humanists. For example, how does the celebration of Diwali from a Hindu perspective compare to a non-religious celebration? This is the time to discuss points such as being with friends and family, different food and wearing new outfits.

Humanist celebrations differ from religious ones because they are not based on worship or divine traditions, but do they share a similar purpose: honouring life's important moments and connecting with others.

Humanists might celebrate seasonal changes like winter solstice, with gatherings focused on gratitude, community and the natural cycle, honouring values like kindness, charity and family (and also linked to the Golden Rules). Religious holidays like Christmas (Christianity), Diwali (Hinduism) and Eid (Islam) also centre around community and gratitude, but often include prayers, specific customs and stories that honour each faith's spiritual perspective.

Class activities
1. **A naming ceremony invite:** Read together as a class the real-life example of a naming ceremony. Discuss the ups and downs of the story and how the story ends with a momentous celebration. Invite the pupils to design and draw an invite for a naming ceremony based on the story. Ask them to include on the invite such things as the Humanism symbol and an explanation of what a naming ceremony is.

2. **Celebration speech creation:** Ask each pupil to think about a loved one whom they'd like to celebrate, such as a family member, friend or teacher. Invite the children to write a short speech expressing why they appreciate their chosen person and what qualities they admire. Compare the pupils' examples to examples from religion, such as a priest who shares sermons with their congregation at church or an imam at a mosque, where they give thanks for God during celebrations such as Christmas and Eid respectively.

Plenary materials
Reiterate to the class what constitutes a happy moment and discuss the similarities and differences between Humanist and religious perspectives.

Recording of learning
Children can write their speeches in their RE books.

16 A worldviews approach

A worldviews approach is something that has become a topic of discussion across all realms of RE and curriculum design.

A worldviews approach in RE emphasises understanding and appreciating diverse perspectives on life's fundamental questions, such as 'What happens when we die?', 'How should we treat others?' and 'What is a good way to live?', encompassing religious and non-religious beliefs. Unlike traditional RE lessons and curriculum design, which have often focused on learning about specific religions in isolation, this approach integrates the study of a wide range of worldviews, including atheism, Humanism and nuances within religions and their followers. It encourages pupils to explore how various beliefs and values shape individuals' identities, practices and ethical decisions. This method promotes critical thinking, empathy and respect for diversity, by enabling pupils to compare and contrast different worldviews, recognise their own biases and understand the dynamic nature of belief systems. In essence, it's all about people, their experiences and how religious and non-religious ways of life are not one-size-fits-all.

By fostering a curious environment where the pupil is at the heart of the learning, the worldviews approach aims to prepare pupils for living in a pluralistic society, enhancing their ability to engage in meaningful dialogue and coexist with others holding different perspectives. Even those from a similar background might challenge each other's thought process – and that's OK! A worldviews approach also emphasises the ever-changing society in which we live and work, allowing for discussions and learning to reflect that.

Organised worldview vs. personal worldview

The Religious Education Council provides the following definitions for an organised worldview and an individual's personal worldview:

- An **organised worldview** can be understood as a 'more or less coherent and established system with certain (written and unwritten) sources, traditions, values, rituals, ideals, or dogmas' (from van der Kooij et al., 2013).
- An individual's **personal worldview** describes and shapes how they encounter, interpret, understand and engage with the world. A person may have a coherent and considered framework for answering questions about the nature of ultimate reality, knowledge, truth and ethics, or they may have never given such questions much thought – but they still have a worldview, including the beliefs, convictions, values and assumptions that influence and shape their thinking and living (Pett, 2024).

It can be seen from these definitions that although different, the two views are also linked – both worldviews play an important role in the teaching and learning of RE.

To expand further, a personal worldview in RE refers to an individual's comprehensive perspective on life, encompassing their beliefs, values, experiences and interpretations of the world. This worldview is shaped by various influences, including cultural background, religious upbringing, personal experiences, education and social interactions. In the context of RE, exploring personal worldviews allows pupils to reflect on their own beliefs and how these shape their understanding of existence, morality and purpose. Continually referring back to the self and pupils' backgrounds helps with deeper discussions and allows pupils to celebrate one another's experiences, as well as learn from one another.

An organised worldview refers to a structured and systematic set of beliefs and practices shared by a community, often embodied in religions like Christianity, Islam or Hinduism. In RE, studying organised worldviews helps pupils to understand how these comprehensive systems shape cultures, influence personal identities and contribute to societal norms and values, fostering a deeper appreciation of global religious diversity. Moreover, it provides the substantive knowledge to then be able to fluidly move from one person's experience to the next, while still understanding practices in different contexts.

What might a worldviews approach look like in primary school?

Key Stage 1

For children in Key Stage 1, incorporating worldviews into RE involves simple, engaging activities that introduce pupils to diverse beliefs and practices in an age-appropriate manner. Storytelling is a powerful tool, using stories from various religious and cultural traditions to highlight different ways in which people understand the world. Through stories, children learn about concepts such as kindness, sharing and respect, which are common across many worldviews. Stories are also an effective teaching tool in Key Stage 2, and provide many opportunities to explore worldviews, not just within RE lessons but across the curriculum.

Hands-on activities like drawing, role-playing and simple crafts can help young children to explore and express different aspects of worldviews. For example, pupils might create art inspired by a festival from another culture or role-play scenarios that teach empathy and cooperation. Songs and music from different traditions can also be a fun way in which to introduce diverse perspectives.

By engaging with worldviews in these ways, children begin to develop an appreciation for diversity, laying the foundation for empathy, respect and curiosity about the world around them.

As always, the person and people are at the heart of the learning. Using case studies (see page 108 for an example) or characters who follow the children through their learning journey from year group to year group would make for a palatable learning experience. Children are able to understand a variety of practices, key pieces of vocabulary and rituals through the lens of one person or character, in many different contexts.

Key Stage 2

For children in Key Stage 2, incorporating worldviews into RE involves more structured activities that encourage deeper engagement with diverse beliefs and practices. At this age, pupils can begin to compare and contrast different worldviews, exploring how they address life's big questions about existence, morality and community.

Interactive lessons, such as discussions, debates and group projects, can help pupils to explore various religious and non-religious perspectives. For example, they might research and present on different festivals, such as Diwali, Hanukkah or Ramadan, learning about the significance of each festival and the values that they promote. Visiting local places of worship or inviting guest speakers from various faiths can provide first-hand insights into different worldviews. This, again, promotes the people element of worldviews.

Through creative writing, children can reflect on their own beliefs and how they relate to those that they study. Encouraging critical thinking and empathy will help pupils to appreciate diversity and develop a more nuanced understanding of the world and its many belief systems.

Case studies and characters that pupils learned about in Key Stage 1 can provide valuable learning opportunities in Key Stage 2. For example, pupils can develop their understanding of how a person might practise in one way, such as routinely attending Sunday school as a Christian, and how this becomes adapted as they become older – for example, attending Church on a Sunday.

Worldviews in the curriculum

In order to be able to gradually weave worldviews into the curriculum, it is important first to understand what this entails and how this may look from key stage to key stage. As discussed, worldviews can be interwoven with what may be considered traditional RE lessons, only this time you are engaging through various lenses and exposing your pupils to more – for example, learning about Eid in Islam and how this looks from different worldviews, such as Muslims in Britain versus Muslims in other countries around the world.

When pupils near the end of Key Stage 2, many SACREs suggest the teaching of Humanism and the introduction of more philosophical questioning, making the study of worldviews more explicit. During this time, introducing comprehensive units on major world religions and secular perspectives, using primary sources, historical contexts and ethical debates, ensures for a flow of teaching and learning at all times. Encouraging independent research projects and facilitating interfaith dialogues or field trips to various places of worship are also ways of approaching your curriculum with a worldviews approach. This ensures a seamless integration of worldviews into the curriculum, fostering a deep, respectful understanding of diverse perspectives as pupils mature.

What can a worldviews approach promote?

A worldviews approach can promote many different skills, including:

1. **Oracy and listening skills:** Oracy and listening skills are vital in RE, especially when approached through diverse worldviews. These skills foster respectful dialogue and deeper understanding among pupils from various cultural and religious backgrounds. Through oracy, pupils are able to articulate their beliefs and practices, enhancing their confidence and communication abilities. Listening skills enable them to genuinely engage with and appreciate different perspectives.
2. **Lived reality:** Incorporating lived reality and experiences into RE enriches learning by making it more relevant and engaging for pupils. This approach emphasises the practical, everyday aspects of religious beliefs and practices, moving beyond theoretical knowledge to explore how faith is experienced in real life. By examining rituals, traditions and personal stories, pupils gain a deeper understanding of how religion shapes identities and communities. This works through all key stages and also offers a curriculum design that creates a clear journey from Key Stage 1 to Key Stage 2.

As you will see in this book, a worldviews approach can be introduced subtly and effectively in the classroom and in your lessons. See, for example, 'How do Humanists celebrate happy moments in life?' (page 102) and 'How do the pillars of Islam help Muslims to plan their lives?' (page 60).

Teaching Primary RE

Case study example

A worldviews approach begins with people. By using a person to study a religion, children have a tangible example for their learning, removing the abstract.

In the example below, our character is Chandeep Kaur – a Sikhi girl who will take the children on a learning journey through Sikhi, via her lens of experiences and practices. The table below would also work well with the Sikhi lessons provided in Chapter 12.

Chandeep Kaur, age ten, is a follower of Sikhi.		
My special places:		My special people:
	Chandeep Kaur	
My special celebrations:		My beliefs/religion:

A worldviews approach

Here, children can reflect on what the character's identity encompasses through their learning. Do they know of Chandeep's religious background? Can they draw on previous learning? Do they celebrate something particular to them or their community? This removes the abstract learning of our new character and adds a real-life context.

The grid below shows an example where the children apply their own name to the same titles; what are their special places, people and celebrations? Just like Chandeep, they also have their worldviews, which are shaped by their experiences.

My special places:		My special people:
	My name	
My special celebrations:		My beliefs/religion:

The character of Chandeep can be applied and continuously referred to throughout the children's learning journey as a reference point. Not only has the abstract been removed, but the knowledge map also becomes a working document for your children to use and edit when new knowledge is discussed and applied.

The learning can begin with your lesson objective: How do Sikhs follow the idea of seva and sangat in British society?

This then leaves you room to build on this idea in subsequent lessons.

Eventually, the knowledge map will become filled with real-life experiences through the character. It also lays down a real-life context each time a new piece of information is studied. Children are able to see the lived reality of these religions. Eventually, the knowledge map may look like this:

My special places: The gurdwara – a holy place for followers of Sikhi to worship in.		My special people: My parents. The Guru at the gurdwara. The Guru Granth Sahib (our holy text).
	Chandeep Kaur	
My special celebrations: Diwali, to celebrate the release of the sixth Guru from prison.		My beliefs/religion: I am a follower of Sikhi. 'Sikh' means student.

This will show the learning journey over time, across varying lessons, in order to obtain this information. This can be a shared class document or individually done by each child.

Another example, using an Abrahamic faith as our centre for learning, is exemplified below.

Saliha Omar is a Muslim girl, who lives with her family in Manchester, England. She is also inviting the children to learn via her day-to-day experiences and what these look like as a Muslim. The table below, again, would be introduced through the Islam lessons and built on gradually.

In the Key Stage 2 lesson 'How do the pillars of Islam help Muslims to plan their lives?' (see page 60), teachers can use the character of Saliha to discuss the Five Pillars, and then add to the 'My beliefs/religion' section how she follows the Five Pillars in her daily life.

My special places: The mosque (previous learning from Key Stage 1).		My special people: My parents. The prophet Muhammad (PBUH).
	Saliha Omar	
My special celebrations: Eid and Ramadan (previous learning from Key Stage 1).		My beliefs/religion: I am a follower of Islam. One of the Five Pillars, zakat, tells me to donate money to charity and those less fortunate than me.

Again, the use of characters allows for pupils to engage with how children similar to them are experiencing life through various religions. It also allows your pupils to use the same concept and reflect on their own lived experiences: do some share the same special places as Saliha if they are a Muslim themselves, for example?

Glossary

General terms

Faith: a strong belief in something, especially without the need for proof or evidence. In a religious context, faith involves a deep trust and belief in the teachings and principles of a particular religion.

Religion: a set of beliefs, practices and values centred around the existence of a higher power or powers. It often includes moral and ethical guidelines for how people should live their lives.

Ritual: a formal and often repetitive set of actions, ceremonies or behaviours performed as part of religious worship or observance. Rituals are symbolic and have special significance within a religious community.

Practice: the actions, customs and behaviours associated with a particular religion. It involves how people express their beliefs in their daily lives.

Abrahamic faiths

Abrahamic: a group of three major religions – Judaism, Christianity and Islam – whose spiritual lineage can be traced back to the biblical figure Abraham. These religions share common historical and religious roots.

Monotheistic: relating to the belief that there is only one God.

Judaism

Judaism: Judaism a religion based on the worship of one God and adherence to the teachings found in the sacred texts, particularly the Torah.

Jewish: an adjective used to describe anything related to Judaism or the Jewish people.

Jew: a noun used to refer to a person who practises Judaism, follows the Jewish faith and/or is part of the Jewish ethnic or religious group. It's important to note that being Jewish can be both a religious and cultural identity.

Abraham: the patriarch and founder of Judaism. He is revered for his unwavering faith in God and his role as the ancestor of the Jewish people. God made a covenant with Abraham, promising him descendants and the land of Canaan.

Hanukkah: Jewish festival lasting eight days, celebrating the rededication of the Second Temple, marked by lighting menorah candles.

Kosher: foods prepared and consumed according to Jewish dietary laws, regulating what is permissible to eat and how it is prepared.

Mitzvah: a commandment or religious duty prescribed by God in the Torah. Mitzvot (plural) encompass a wide range of ethical, ritual and ceremonial obligations that guide Jewish life and practice.

Moses: a significant figure, revered as a prophet, lawgiver and leader. Moses led the Israelites out of slavery in Egypt, received the Ten Commandments from God on Mount Sinai and guided the Israelites during their journey in the wilderness.

Passover: Jewish holiday commemorating the Israelites' Exodus from Egypt, celebrated with a special meal (Seder) and symbolic foods.

Rabbi: a Jewish religious leader and teacher, often responsible for leading services, offering spiritual guidance and teaching the Torah.

Sabbath (Shabbat): the Jewish day of rest, from Friday evening to Saturday evening, dedicated to worship, rest and family time. Shabbat is the Hebrew word for Saturday and the Sabbath. Candles are lit on Friday evening to welcome Shabbat.

Synagogue: Jewish places of worship and community gathering, where services, prayers and educational activities take place.

Talmud: a collection of Jewish texts, consisting of the Mishnah (oral laws) and Gemara (commentary). It elaborates on the Torah and guides Jewish law, ethics and practice.

Tanakh: the Hebrew Bible, consisting of three parts: Torah (Law), Nevi'im (Prophets) and Ketuvim (Writings). It is central to Jewish religious teachings and traditions.

Torah: the most sacred text in Judaism, containing the divine laws and teachings revealed to Moses by God. It consists of the first five books of the Hebrew Bible, which are known as Genesis, Exodus, Leviticus, Numbers and Deuteronomy.

Christianity

Christianity: a monotheistic religion based on the life and teachings of Jesus Christ. It emphasises faith, love and salvation and is rooted in the belief in the Holy Trinity – Father, Son and Holy Spirit. The Bible serves as the sacred scripture, guiding Christian beliefs and practices.

Christian: an adherent of Christianity, and someone who follows the teachings of Jesus Christ. Christians believe in the divinity of Jesus, salvation through faith and living by moral and ethical principles outlined in the Bible.

Crucifix: a cross, often with a figure of Jesus on it. It reminds Christians of Jesus's crucifixion, where he was nailed to a cross. It's a symbol of love and sacrifice for Christians, representing Jesus's death and resurrection.

Disciples: followers or students who learned from Jesus and who became his close friends.

Jesus Christ: the central figure in Christianity, believed by Christians to be the Son of God and the Saviour. His teachings on love, compassion and salvation form the basis of Christian rules. The crucifixion and resurrection of Jesus are pivotal events in Christian theology.

Parable: a simple story that teaches a lesson, as told by Jesus.
Resurrection: in relation to Christianity, Jesus's coming back to life after death.
Saviour: a reference to Jesus Christ. Christians believe that he sacrificed himself in order to make salvation possible for human beings.

Islam

Islam: a monotheistic religion founded on the teachings of Prophet Muhammad (PBUH) and rooted in the belief in Allah.
Muslim: A Muslim is a follower of Islam, adhering to its beliefs and practices, such as prayer and charity.

Allah: the Arabic word for God in Islam. Muslims believe in the oneness of Allah, emphasising His attributes of compassion, mercy and omnipotence. It is a direct transliteration from Arabic to English, rather than the name of a god.
Eid: a festive celebration in Islam marking the end of Ramadan. It includes special prayers, feasts and giving to charity. Eid al-Fitr and Eid al-Adha are significant Eid celebrations in Islam.
The Five Pillars of Islam are fundamental: shahada (declaration of faith), salah (or salat) (prayer five times a day), zakat (charitable giving), sawm (fasting during Ramadan) and hajj (pilgrimage to Mecca once in a lifetime).
The Hajj: a pilgrimage to the holy city of Mecca that Muslims try to make at least once in their lifetime. It involves rituals like circling the Kaaba and praying.
The Kaaba: a sacred building located in Mecca, Saudi Arabia, and the holiest site in Islam. It is a cube-shaped building draped in black cloth, believed to have been built by Prophet Abraham. Muslims face the Kaaba during prayers and visit it during the Hajj.
Iman: faith or belief in Islam. Having strong iman means having confidence in Allah's wisdom and mercy. Iman is an essential part of being Muslim and shapes how Muslims live their lives.
Makkah/Mecca: the holiest city in Islam, in Saudi Arabia. Muslims face towards Mecca when they pray. It's the destination of the Hajj and holds great significance.
Minaret: a tower in mosques, which signifies the call to prayer and the connection between heaven and earth.
Prophet Muhammad (SAW/PBUH): Islam's final messenger, receiving revelations from Allah. The spelling of his name in English can vary – for example, Mohammad, Mohammed – reflecting transliteration differences from Arabic. 'PBUH' stands for 'peace be upon him', a respectful phrase used by Muslims after mentioning prophets, especially Prophet Muhammad. The meaning of the Arabic phrase *sallallahu alayhi wa sallam* (abbreviation SAW) is 'may Allah honour him and grant him peace' or 'peace and blessings of Allah be upon him'.
Quran: the holy book of Islam, written in Arabic and believed by Muslims to be the word of God as revealed to Prophet Muhammad (PBUH). It contains guidance on moral, spiritual and practical aspects of life, serving as a fundamental source of wisdom and instruction for Muslims.

Ramadan: the Islamic holy month of fasting, prayer and reflection. During Ramadan, Muslims fast from dawn to sunset, refraining from food and drink. It's a time for spiritual growth, charity and community, ending with the celebration of Eid al-Fitr, a joyful festival marking the month's completion.

Ummah: the community of Muslims around the world. It can be thought of as a big family where everyone supports and cares for each other. Muslims feel a strong bond with fellow members of the ummah, united by their faith in Allah and the teachings of Islam.

Dharmic faiths

Dharma: the natural order of the universe, encompassed through duty, righteousness and moral law. It guides individuals to live ethically and fulfil their responsibilities in society according to divine order. Each living thing is living out its own path through dharma.

Karma: the law of cause and effect. Actions performed in this life influence future experiences and determine one's destiny in subsequent lives. Good deeds can lead to positive outcomes in this life or the next, while bad deeds can lead to suffering.

Reincarnation: the belief that the soul undergoes a series of births and deaths, moving from one body to another in a cycle of rebirths until it achieves liberation (moksha).

Hinduism/Sanatana Dharma

Hinduism/Sanatana Dharma: Hinduism is characterised by its reverence for a multitude of deities, rituals, compassion for growth and sacred texts, such as the Vedas, Upanishads and Bhagavad Gita. The name Hinduism comes from the Indus River. Followers often refer to it as 'Sanatana Dharma' (the 'eternal way').

Avatar: divine incarnations of gods on Earth to restore dharma and righteousness.

Brahman: the supreme universal spirit, the ultimate reality and the source of all existence.

Incarnation: the manifestation of a deity or divine being in a physical form on Earth. Examples include Vishnu incarnating as Rama or Krishna.

Trimurti: the triad of Hindu deities, representing the three cosmic functions: Brahma (creation), Vishnu (preservation) and Shiva (transformation). They symbolise the cyclical nature of existence.

Vedas: ancient sacred texts of Hinduism, composed in the ancient language of Sanskrit. They contain hymns, rituals, philosophy and spiritual wisdom, serving as the foundation of Dharmic religious knowledge and practice.

Sikhism – Sikh Dharma

Sikhi: the religion followed by Sikhs. It teaches love, equality and service to others. Sikhs believe in one God (Ik Onkar) and follow the teachings of the Sikh Gurus.

Gurdwara: a Sikh place of worship. It is where Sikhs gather to pray, sing hymns and listen to the teachings of the Guru Granth Sahib. Gurdwaras also serve free meals to all visitors as a symbol of equality and community. The kitchen within the gurdwara is called a langar.

Guru Granth Sahib: the holy scripture of Sikhi. It is a collection of hymns and writings by Sikh Gurus and other saints. Sikhs regard the Guru Granth Sahib as their eternal Guru and show it great respect in gurdwaras and in their homes.

Guru Nanak: the founder of Sikhi and the first of the ten Sikh Gurus. He was born in 1469 AD in present-day Pakistan and taught about peace, unity and compassion.

The Five Ks: five articles of faith that Sikhs wear as symbols of their identity and devotion to their religion. They include **kesh** (uncut hair), **kara** (steel bracelet), **kanga** (wooden comb), **kachera** (cotton undergarment) and **kirpan** (ceremonial sword).

Buddhism

Buddha: the founder of Buddhism. His real name was Siddhartha Gautama and he is known as the 'Enlightened One'.

Enlightenment: a state of perfect wisdom and peace that Buddhists aim to achieve.

Four Noble Truths: the main ideas of Buddhism that explain why people suffer and how to stop suffering: suffering; the cause of suffering; the end of suffering; the path to end suffering.

Karma: the belief that good actions bring good results and bad actions bring bad results.

Meditation: a practice where people sit quietly and focus their minds to become calm and aware.

Noble Eightfold Path: the steps that Buddhists follow to live a good and peaceful life. These include being kind, telling the truth and meditating.

Reincarnation: the idea that when someone dies, they are born again in a new life.

Jainism

Jainism: an ancient religion that originated in India, focusing on non-violence, truth and spiritual purity. Followers of Jainism are called Jains.

Ahimsa: non-violence or not harming any living being. It is a central principle in Jainism, encouraging Jains to live peacefully and avoid causing harm to animals, plants and even insects.

Tirthankara: a spiritual teacher in Jainism who has achieved enlightenment and helps others to reach the same state. There have been 24 Tirthankaras, with Mahavira being the most well-known.

Other approaches

Agnostic: a person who believes that the existence of gods or deities is unknown or unknowable, remaining open to the possibility but without firm belief or disbelief.

Atheist: a person who does not believe in the existence of any gods or deities, often relying on science and reason for understanding the world.

Autonomy: the principle of self-governance and making informed decisions independently, highlighting personal responsibility and freedom in Humanist ideology.

Empathy: the ability to understand and share the feelings of others, promoting compassionate and ethical interactions in Humanist values.

Ethics: a system of moral principles guiding human conduct, emphasising human welfare, fairness and justice, without reliance on religious beliefs.

Humanism: an approach emphasising reason, ethics and human welfare, focusing on secular and scientific approaches to understanding life.

Reason: the use of logical thinking and evidence-based understanding to make decisions and solve problems, central to Humanist ideas.

Secular: pertaining to attitudes, activities or other things that have no religious or spiritual basis, crucial in Humanist thought.

Bibliography

Department for Children, Schools and Families (DCSF) (2010), 'Religious education in English schools: Non-statutory guidance 2010', https://assets.publishing.service.gov.uk/media/5a7adb3ce5274a34770e7953/DCSF-00114-2010.pdf

Diocese of Lincoln Board of Education (2021), 'Assessing progress in RE: Guidance', www.lincolndiocesaneducation.com/attachments/download.asp?file=347&type=pdf

Pett, S. (2024), 'Developing a religion and worldviews approach in religious education in England: A handbook for curriculum writers', The RE Council of England and Wales Religion and Worldviews Project, https://religiouseducationcouncil.org.uk/rec/wp-content/uploads/2024/04/24-25698-REC-Handbook-A4-DIGITAL-PAGES.pdf

Religious Education Council (2023), 'National Content Standard for RE released', https://religiouseducationcouncil.org.uk/2023/09/national-content-standard-for-re-released

RE Today (n.d.), 'SACRE/LA: Agreed syllabus for RE', www.retoday.org.uk/consultancy/sacre-la

van der Kooij, C. J., de Ruyter, D. J. and Miedema, S. (2013), '"Worldview": The meaning of the concept and the impact on religious education', *Religious Education*, 108, (2), 210–228.

All the books in the Bloomsbury Curriculum Basics series

Bloomsbury Curriculum Basics: Teaching Primary French
Amanda Barton & Angela McLachlan | 9781472920683

Bloomsbury Curriculum Basics: Teaching Primary Spanish
Amanda Barton & Angela McLachlan | 9781472920713

Bloomsbury Curriculum Basics: Teaching Primary Art and Design
Emily Gopaul | 9781472945914

Bloomsbury Curriculum Basics: Teaching Primary PE
Jazz Rose | 9781472921055

Revised editions

Bloomsbury Curriculum Basics: Teaching Primary Science
Peter Riley | 9781801993913

Bloomsbury Curriculum Basics: Teaching Primary History
Matthew Howorth | 9781801993883

Bloomsbury Curriculum Basics: Teaching Primary Geography
Stephen Scoffham & Paula Owens | 9781801993982

Bloomsbury Curriculum Basics: Teaching Primary Computing
Martin Burrett | 9781801993968